Mastering the Net:
Field Hockey Goalkeeping Basics

Erica Johnson-Crell

Wish Publishing
Terre Haute, Indiana
www.wishpublishing.com

Edited by Heather Lowhorn
Editorial assistance provided by Dorothy Chambers
Cover designed by Phil Velikan
Cover photography © 2005 Rich Clarkson and Associates

Printed in the United States of America
10 9 8 7 6 5 4 3 2 1

Published in the United States by
Wish Publishing
P.O. Box 10337
Terre Haute, IN 47801, USA
www.wishpublishing.com

Distributed in the United States by
Cardinal Publishers Group
2222 Hillside Avenue, Suite 100
Indianapolis, Indiana 46218
www.cardinalpub.com

Dedicated to:

My husband, the love of my life, for his constant support and for inspiring me to inspire others; and my family and friends for believing in me.

Acknowledgements

Writing a book is never an easy task, but with the help of friends and family it can be made easier. I am grateful to a number of people who helped to make this book possible. I would like to thank Lauren Adejuwon for putting me in contact with Wish Publishing. I would like to extend a big thank you to Lebanon Valley College for providing the facility for photographs and to Laurel Martin and the Lebanon Valley College field hockey coaching staff for being big supporters. A big thank you goes to Katie Pawlewicz for her willingness to model the skills and techniques portrayed in the demonstration photographs. A special thank you to my husband, Barry Crell, for providing his photography expertise and to Joe del Tufo for his digital art expertise. Thanks to Jim Haven for his art drawing expertise on the drills in the appendix. I'd especially like to thank my former teammates and coaches who helped make this game so special to me. Lastly, it would not be right if I didn't thank the one person who introduced the game to me and who was a major influence on my field hockey career — Barbara Thompson. I am thankful not only for her willingness to write the foreword for this book, but also for her encouragement of my skills. I hope in some way this book will help to excite others and influence their careers as she has done for me.

Foreword

When one throws a pebble into a lake, it is amazing to see how far the ripples travel. And so it is with no surprise that this book would be a ripple result of granting a simple favor. It was about the second week of school, and I was just finishing plans for the day's practice when I heard a knock at the door and a hearty "Yo, can you do me a favor?" So I responded, "Sure, if you do one for me." The favor was giving Erica her locker combination. It was given, the locker opened, and she returned to my office and asked, "Okay, now what can I do for you?"

And so that same afternoon, despite not knowing anything about field hockey and trusting that we would teach her, Erica arrived at the fields. After the other goalies helped her to get suited up, she walked over to the goal, turned, and assumed one of the best ready positions I had seen in my years involved in coaching.

That season was a learning experience for Erica — the skills, the techniques, the angles, the offense, the defense, the rules (no, you can't grab the ball and throw it). As Erica discusses in her introduction, the one thing that never had to be taught was desire. She possessed a desire to be the best. She turned that desire into reality two years later as a senior when she recorded 210 saves and allowed only 10 goals. She was selected First Team All Conference, All Group IV, Senior All Star, and First Team All State.

While I wish I could take credit for all her accolades, I cannot. She and her family made the commitment to become involved in the Future's Program where Erica received outstanding instruction and improved her ability to "execute skills with precision, speed, and without hesitation."

She continued her growth in college at Old Dominion and Rutgers, before injuries ended her playing career. Her love of the game continued as Erica was actively recruited to work camps and clinics and to stay with the Future's Program as a coach. She continued to come back to West and work with our goalies — sometimes suiting up to demonstrate, sometimes in her suit and heels from work.

Erica's exuberance for teaching, her desire to help others be successful, her willingness to share her knowledge and experiences were given to our goalies and are now captured in this book. Whether she is discussing equipment, technique, drills or mindset, her enthusiasm for the game ripples on every page. A player just starting, an experienced player or a coach could greatly benefit from reading this book.

Barbara J. Thompson
Teacher, Coach
Cherry Hill West High School

Table of Contents

chapter 1

Mental Toughness

Introduction

Great achievements start with desire and then become reality. In sports, desire needs to be more than hoping or wishing for success. It is inner strength and focused commitment that turns desire into reality. A goalkeeper must possess this desire and inner strength to achieve greatness in the goal. A goalkeeper's mindset is different than that of a field player's. A goalkeeper must possess excellent physical and mental qualities and proper technique to achieve the dream of success.

Being a goalkeeper requires strong mental ability. A mind is the most valuable piece of equipment that a goalkeeper possesses. She must be able to remain calm, make quick decisions, and be able to play the ball under pressure. The circle is her domain, and she has to take charge of it. The goalkeeper is the leader of the circle and the defense must work with her to prevent a goal.

A good goalkeeper will be able to read the game, direct defense and position herself. She has the best view, so she should be doing most of the directing in the backfield. Understanding the role of defense will enhance her ability to organize the unit with leadership, apply proper techniques and protect the goal. A goalkeeper should start directing her defense and moving her defenders into position from approximately the 25-yard line to goal line. A goalkeeper should be able to focus on and see all areas of the field, even the area that is behind her. It takes skill and practice to be able to move, direct defense, watch the play, and anticipate passes and moves of the attacker.

Attitude/Confidence

The keys to being a goalkeeper are attitude and confidence. That is why they say goalkeepers are born and not made. Your strongest players should be the center forward and the goalkeeper. They are the glue of the team. They dictate the tone of play and the type of play that needs to be executed by their team. Attitude is important in winning the mind game. When a goalkeeper has a strong, positive attitude, her teammates and attackers sense that confidence. That confidence can help position the team in a successful playing situation. Winning the mind game is when you convince your attacker that you are stronger, better and faster than she is. If your attacker thinks you are, then you are. The attacker loses her own confidence because your attitude is stronger and more intimidating.

The hard part of the mind game is actually convincing your goalkeeper that she is all these things. A goalkeeper's confidence level must be extremely high. Your goalkeeper should have the attitude that she is always going to win. If an athlete isn't confident when she steps into the goal, the skills will be executed with hesitation instead of precision and speed. A goalkeeper must believe she is a wall in front of the goal. Of course, the occasional ball will pass by and score; it's bound to happen. But a goalkeeper with a good attitude will shrug it off and continue to play her best. It is attitude that elevates an athlete from a good player to an excellent player.

One piece of advice though: don't let your goalkeeper become so confident that she takes her attacker for granted. There is a fine line between confidence and arrogance. Don't let your goalkeeper take anyone for granted. Her attackers are working just as hard as she is, if not harder. Make sure your goalkeeper stays focused while in the goal.

What Is a goalkeeper?

A goalkeeper is a quick decision-maker who is responsible for directing the entire field. A goalkeeper's baseline skills supplement her natural athletic instinct. Her head should be up and her eyes should be aware of her surroundings. The ball must go through 10 other people before it gets to the goalkeeper, but the goalkeeper is the last line of defense before the ball can go into the goal. That's why this position is the most important position on the field, and it should be treated as such.

A great goalkeeper is distinguished from a good goalkeeper by her quick and confident choices. She must be quick at making decisions in three categories: angles, clears and saves. A goalkeeper must be able to make decisions in a split second and possibly reevaluate that decision when the situation changes. This is where the aspect of natural ability comes into play. A goalkeeper must be able to instantly think of her next move while executing the current move. A natural goalkeeper will often apply skills from other sports or intertwine basic skills.

Most goalkeepers are extremely physical and possess strong psychological qualities. A goalkeeper needs strength, agility, flexibility, explosiveness, coordination, quickness, speed, balance, endurance, courage, creativity and concentration. There is a lot of pressure on a goalkeeper to get the job done and keep the ball out of the goal, so the qualities of strength, courage, attitude and concentration are important.

chapter 2

Gearing Up

Goalkeepers have to protect their bodies as much as they can. Having quality equipment is essential in providing that protection. The equipment can be expensive, but it important to keep safety first by providing full protection. Basic equipment includes foot guards, leg guards, hip protectors with a built-in pelvic protector, chest protector, gloves, throat protector and a helmet (Figure 1A).

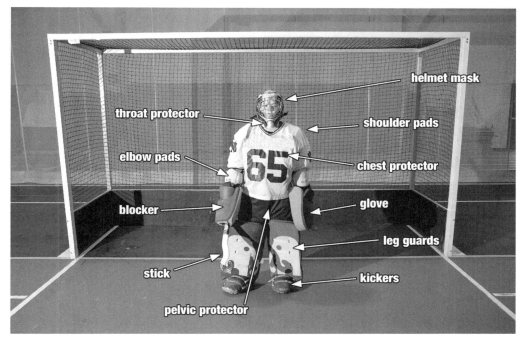

Figure 1A.

Even with all that protection, the ball will still find the areas on the body that don't have padding. Most goalkeepers add supplemental equipment with extra accessories to protect them as much as possible. Higher-level goalkeepers wear shoulder pads, elbow pads, pelvic protectors,

Figure 1B

kneepads, and shin guards worn backward to protect the calf (Figure 1B). When fully equipped and protected, the goalkeeper has a greater chance of stopping the ball and executing the play without getting hurt.

Sticks

There are several different types of sticks out there for a goalkeeper to use. Finding one that is right for your goalkeeper depends on size and arm strength. If your goalkeeper has strong arms, a field player's stick may be better for her to use. These have a tendency to be heavier, and your goalkeeper may feel more secure with a stick with weight in her hands. However, if your goalkeeper doesn't have strong arms or she doesn't feel comfortable with a field player's stick, there are molded sticks for goalkeepers. Lighter and flatter than a field player's stick, a goalkeeper's stick has a dramatic hook and often a groove in the shaft so that the goalkeeper's hands can fit securely around the shaft of the stick. The key is to choose a stick that is right for your goalkeeper — something that will feel comfortable in her hands all day long.

Blocker

The blocker is a protective covering over the stick hand. When the goalkeeper is playing the ball, the blocker is another piece of equipment that she has to protect herself. The blocker can be used, like the glove, to deflect the ball, but it is mainly used to protect the hand for a secure and safe grip on the stick. There are several different types of blockers. There are foam padding blockers with protective covering. It is necessary for your goalkeeper to choose a piece of equipment that she is comfortable with and that fits her level of play.

Glove

The glove is a handy piece of equipment. Like the blocker, it is used to deflect the ball. The glove is used in many situations. When down on the ground, it can be used to deflect flicks or scoops. It is used to get aerials that the feet cannot reach, and it is used to cover more space as an extension of the arm. Like most pieces of equipment, there are several different kinds of gloves. Some gloves have more foam padding than others and are recommended for the safety of your goalkeeper. A glove that is made of the same material as the leg guards and kickers is also recommended, because it will not only protect your goalkeeper, but it will allow her to do a variety of things with the ball in the air. However, please be sure that your goalkeeper knows the proper technique before using this type of glove. This type of glove can propel a ball like the kickers and leg pads do. Therefore, for the safety of the field players, it is recommended that beginner goalkeepers use nonpropel-foam gloves. These gloves are well-padded with a leather seal, which is lighter and easier to move with the goalkeeper. These gloves are great for directing the ball and moving it to a position where it can be kicked out of the zone. The last type of glove, which is not recommended, is much like a soccer goalkeeper glove. There is not much padding at all, with a leather seal. These gloves were widely used years ago, but I rarely see them today. However, if you do have these gloves, they should only be used for training purposes. The fingers of this glove can be curled and moved, so they can help a goalkeeper to catch the ball. As a beginning goalkeeper, catching the ball will help develop eye-hand coordination. But with the lack of padding that these gloves provide, a goalkeeper could get hurt at any level of play when trying to deflect a ball with these gloves. Please do not use them in live play.

Helmet Mask and Throat Protector

There are several types of helmet masks. As in most sports, the safety and style of helmet masks are evolving. Newer helmet masks look more like ice hockey helmet masks than the standard field hockey ones. I recommend that a high-level goalkeeper invest in one of these new helmet masks. I also recommend being especially cautious when choosing a helmet mask. It is important that the helmet mask fits snugly, but not so tightly that it creates a headache. It should be tight enough that when a goalkeeper dives on the ground, the helmet mask is able to stay on her head. It should have adjustable bolts for tightening and loosening the helmet for this purpose. For the safety of the goalkeeper, it is important to choose not the cheapest helmet mask, but the safest. Since goalkeepers are on the ground making extensive dives and dangerous saves, you want them to have the best protection for their heads. Likewise, the throat is a vulnerable area that can be easily damaged by a ball or stick. Therefore, throat protection should always be worn. The construction of throat protectors is pretty standard — plastic with cotton cloth covering and Velcro clasps that close in the back of the neck.

Hip Pads and Pelvic Protector

Hip protectors protect the upper quadriceps, pelvis, coccyx bone and hips from a hard shot that cannot be stopped by the legs. Some hip protectors have more padding than others, but any type will protect a goalkeeper. Pelvic protectors are a necessary piece of equipment for any goalkeeper, male or female. A hard shot that comes in contact with an unprotected pelvic area can do damage; therefore, it is necessary to protect this area.

Leg Guards

Leg guards are the most important pieces of equipment for the goalkeeper. They are used in almost every skill that the goalkeeper executes. They come in all shapes and sizes. Years ago, leg guards were made of flexible canvas with hard plastic or bamboo poles across the shin area. They were called "canes." Some high schools that play on grass still use these today. But due to the weight of these leg guards, they tend to throw the goalkeeper's weight back and slow down the goalkeeper's sprinting and reaction time. Today most middle and high schools and colleges use Styrofoam leg guards. The best way to choose a leg guard is by style and function. Some leg guards are geared for different types of surfaces. When choosing a leg guard, it is best to find one that the goalkeeper is comfortable with. The new leg guards mold to the goalkeeper's legs and are more aerodynamic. Leg guards vary in weight but in general are not that heavy. A goalkeeper should choose leg guards according to skill level, comfort and fit.

Kickers

The kickers are an essential part of the goalkeeper's equipment. They are used in almost every skill the goalkeeper executes. Years ago, kickers were made of flexible canvas and were strapped around the ankle and under the foot with reinforced toes called "domain kickers." These kickers accompanied the canes. Like the canes, however, these kickers were heavy and tended to throw the goalkeeper's weight back on her heels. Today most schools and colleges use the Styrofoam kickers. Either way, choosing a kicker that is best for the goalkeeper is the main concern. Like the leg guards, these are made for different surfaces and for different types of shoes. It is best to choose kickers that match the leg guards, not only for style, but also for comfort. The goalkeeper is the one wearing them, so she should be comfortable with them.

Chest Protector

There are many types of chest protectors, but they all have a common purpose: to protect the chest area. Stomach protectors and shoulder protectors should also be used. The stomach protector protects just the stomach and chest area, but leaves the shoulders and arms vulnerable. Therefore, a shoulder protector on top of the stomach protector will help to safeguard all vulnerable upper-body areas.

Optional Equipment

There are several optional pieces of equipment that a high-level goalkeeper should invest in for more protection. Cloth shin guards worn backward on the calf will protect the goalkeeper in splits and slides on turf or grass. Also, elbow pads and wrist guards will help the goalkeeper prevent bruises and cuts while doing slides and dives. Kneepads can be used to protect the vulnerable part of the knee that is not protected by leg guards or hip protectors while going down into a slide tackle.

Supply Bag

Every goalkeeper should have an emergency supply bag inside her equipment bag. The supply bag will keep her prepared for every situation. The supply bag should include the following:

- Screwdriver—for tightening and loosening screws on helmet mask

- Pad buckles—spare buckles for leg guards

- Straps—spare straps for leg guards and kickers

- Tape (duck tape, athletic tape, and shoo-goo)—for repair and maintenance of equipment

- Screws—spare screws for helmet mask

- Foam—extra padding for inside a glove

- Bandages (prewrap, adhesive bandages, headband)— for those first aid needs

---

Each of these pieces of equipment will help to gear a more confident and aggressive goalkeeper. Extra protection is always recommended; however, these options are not required.

chapter 3

Roles/Responsibilities

The goalkeeper is the nerve center of the team. She is the only player with the entire field in front of her, so she is the "eyes" of the team. What she says and how she says it is just as important as what she does. Consequently, there must be trust and confidence between her and the defense.

The Three C's of Goalkeeping

In order for a goalkeeper to be successful in her team defense role, she must follow the three C's of goalkeeping — courage, concentration, and communication.

Courage

Courage is needed to successfully meet challenges and to be fearless in defense of the goal. The goalkeeper should possess the confidence to dominate the circle by verbally taking charge, demanding the ball, and playing attackers. When a crucial mistake occurs, a goalkeeper must not let it affect that confidence. A good goalkeeper has courage because she is always mentally prepared for a game.

Concentration

Concentration involves the ability to focus total attention on a specific task. Concentration is especially important in the defensive circle. Remember, the circle is the goalkeeper's domain; she should keep focused on it. To stay focused, she should know where the ball is at all times and where all attackers and defenders are between the 25-yard line and the goal line. The goalkeeper should have the ability to anticipate the play. Concentration and anticipation can be keys to solid defensive play, not only in the circle, but anywhere on the field. A goalkeeper should focus her attention on the position of the ball, movement of the attackers, and organization of the defense.

Communication

A goalkeeper needs to be clear and firm in communicating to her defense. It is the goalkeeper's job to keep the team composed and ready for every situation. Composure and effective communication during the game can reduce stress, confusion and goals allowed. The goalkeeper should use clear and quick words to communicate with the defense. It is important to note that occasionally a goalkeeper may need to yell to convey urgency. This should never be confused with a personal attack. The following are examples of words that should be used by a goalkeeper:

Pressure	I have ball	Out	Coming on
Hard right/left	Shot	Mine	Cover
Force left/right	Stay mark	Go	Bring her
Mark	Keeper	Drop	Go to ball
Time	Outside right/left	Shift	

Table 1.

Practice Roles

Practice Warm-ups

Even though field hockey is a team sport, a goalkeeper has different skills from the rest of the team, so she is often isolated. A goalkeeper rarely warms up with the team. Some teams have the goalkeeper stretch and run with the team, but for time's sake it is best to train the goalkeeper separately so that when the team is done warming up, the goalkeeper is ready to move into shooting drills. A goalkeeper should go through several different warm-ups before putting on her equipment.

1. Warm up to increase heart rate

2. Stretch

3. Plyometrics

4. Footwork (see Appendix A for some examples)

5. Put on equipment

6. Warm up (see Appendix B for some examples)

7. Break into game-like situations

8. Work with team

Game Warm-ups

Game warm-up is different than practice. A goalkeeper should arrive 15 minutes before the team, if possible. While running laps, she should inspect the goal areas. If playing on grass, she should look for divots, mud trails, rocks and hills. If playing on artificial turf, she should take a look at the pitch angle. Some turfs have different rolls and stitches than others. Every field is different and have different advantages and disadvantages. All these factors can make the ball move differently. If she prepares herself and knows that these factors are in her area, she'll be ready for any situation that could occur because of the surface. Depending on the time allotted for the warm-up, a goalkeeper should try to do everything on the list that she does in practice.

Practice Example

The following list is an example of what a typical practice should look like. This is just a guide and by no means should be considered an authoritative practice layout. You should tailor your practices to what your team and goalkeeper most need to focus on. The following are just suggestions to keep you on the right track.

WARM-UP

RUN

(4+ laps around the field at an easy pace to increase heart rate and warm up the muscles)

STRETCH

PLYOMETRICS

(for goalkeepers focus on butt kicks, side slides, high knees and accelerated/decelerated runs)

FOOTWORK

W-Breakdown/W-Run/The Wave

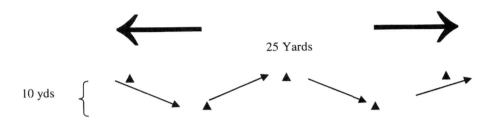

25 Yards

10 yds

Figure 2. W-Breakdown:

- Start at end cone

- Accelerate to each cone, break down, drop step, and sprint to next cone, etc.

- Stay low and on the toes, pump arms through the run, open hips on drop step toward the next cone

W-Run:

- Start at end cone

- Accelerate to each cone and drop step in a continuous run through each cone

- Sprint through the cones, pump arms, stay low and on the toes, open hips on drop step and turn

The Wave:

- Start at end cone

- Sprint, backpedal, sprint, backpedal through the cones

Spider

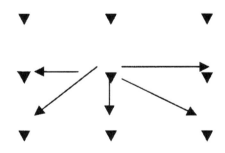

Figure 3.

- Facing forward, sprint or slide to each cone

- Vary your pattern

GET WATER/PUT EQUIPMENT ON
SHOOTING WARMUP

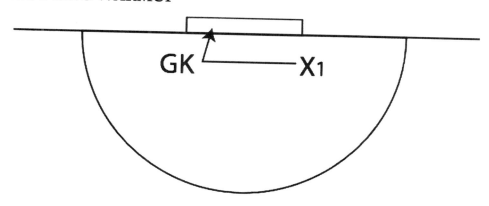

Figure 4. X sends the ball by push pass or hit to the goalkeeper. The goalkeeper works on crossovers and redirects into the goal. Balls should be placed at the 5-yard hash end line area outside the goal. Switch sides to work on both legs.

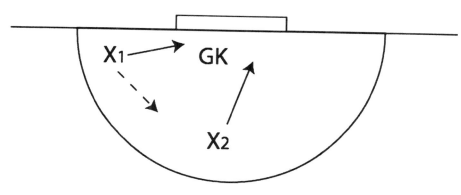

Figure 5. X1 can pass to X2 or shoot at the goalkeeper from Zone 3. The goalkeeper must try to intercept the pass or deflect the shot over the end line or in a space. Emphasize using the non-post leg for clears.

BREAK AWAY FOR WORK WITH TEAM

chapter 4

Positioning/Angles for Maximum Coverage

The key aspects of the goalkeeper's performance are positioning and angle from post to post. A goalkeeper's skills can be excellent, but if her positioning is incorrect she will be beaten by her attacker.

Position the goalkeeper so that she is facing the ball squarely in the center of the goal. The goalkeeper must always remain in front of the goal. She should be five yards in front of the goalmouth, directly behind the stroke mark. The farther out a goalkeeper plays, the more narrow the angle for the attacker—and the more vulnerable the goal behind her. The aim of the goalkeeper is to give the smallest view of the goal to the attacker while giving herself enough time to react.

Angles are very important to the goalkeeper and the attacker. By increasing the distance from the goalmouth, the goalkeeper decreases the angle at which the attacker has to score a goal. To emphasize this point, place the goalkeeper on the goal line and the ball at the top of the circle. Now you can see that the goalkeeper has to take more steps to either side of her to cover the goalmouth.

With the correct angles, the goalkeeper narrows down the shot on goal for the attacker. The attacker is either forced to fire the ball right at the goalkeeper's leg guards or pass it to another attacker. The positioning of the goalkeeper can be tricky. She doesn't want to be too far away from the goal and make it vulnerable for a one-touch past the goalkeeper for a goal, but she doesn't want to be too close and leave the corners of the goal vulnerable. I suggest five to seven yards out from the goalmouth with possible confident advances toward the attacker. The majority of the time, however, the goalkeeper will be holding her position and patiently waiting for her opportunity to perform a skill. As she becomes more comfortable with the position, she will find a comfortable place that best fits her abilities.

The goalkeeper uses short, quick steps to maintain the distance between the ball and the center of the goal. She should be in a set position (see stance in Chapter 5). Use the stroke mark as a reference for where the center of the field and goal are located behind the goalkeeper. When on the move, a goalkeeper should be able to gauge her position on the field using her peripheral vision, the stroke mark and the goal posts. From this position her angles are like a triangle (Figure 6). The goalkeeper follows the ball up and down the goal area with small, swift, hip pivot turns to the sides. To understand angles, have the goalkeeper stand at the stroke mark and draw an imaginary line from the ball, through her legs, and to the center of the goal (Figure 7). This is termed "square to the ball" or "on angle." In this position she should be one equally large step away from covering the goal on either side. If the ball is hit outside this large step, then it is wide of the goal.

The point of all this is to protect the goal and to make sure it is always covered with at least one movement. Remind your goalkeeper to keep her movements short, but explosive.

If you haven't noticed, field hockey is about geometric shapes. A field player always wants to be sure that her through- and flat-passes are covered so her players form a triangle to create this. Goalkeepers must do the same. A triangle is a part of her angle. If you draw a line from one post to the ball, from the other post to the ball, and between the two

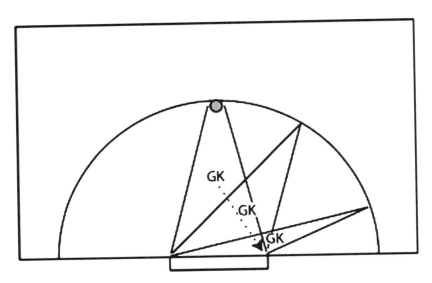

Figure 6. This is a movement that a goalkeeper should make around the goal with the ball. This also shows how the goalkeeper can cover the goal when the ball is at different positions.

posts, you have a triangle. Goalkeepers want to stay within this triangle to be on angle (Figure 6). Do not let the goalkeeper round out to the ball, or her triangle will be unaligned. Instead, have her open her hips and point her toes to the goal post or stroke mark and "square out" (meaning turn and face the ball). As she adjusts to the movement and the ball moves faster, she will need to shuffle (side slide) or turn and sprint, then square out. For a beginner, move slowly through this process. Start with opening her hips and facing the ball, then progress to the turn and sprint (Figure 8).

When a goalkeeper is out of position to play the ball successfully, she gets beaten. She should always know where she is in relation to the goal, because if she does, she will know if a shot is wide without having to look behind her for reference. She must be able to mentally draw lines from the ball to the posts and bisect the angle. Make sure that your goalkeeper is playing the ball not the attacker. She moves in a triangle in front of the goal and uses the stroke mark as a reference point (Figure 6).

Angles take constant work and practice, as well as reinforcement by the coach. But take note that each goalkeeper is going to tailor some skills. This doesn't make them wrong. The idea here is to provide the goalkeepers with the basic skills. So long as they use the basic skills, how they adapt them to create their own is fine.

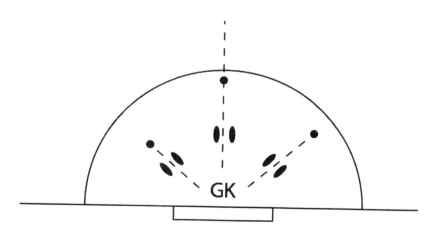

Figure 7. This is an example of the positioning the goalkeeper should have for positions of the ball. Have your goalkeeper draw an imaginary line from the ball, between her legs, and to the center of the goal. If this line is straight and she is bisecting the line with her feet, then she is on the correct angle.

The Dance: Cha-Cha-Cha

Have your goalkeeper maintain the ready position when she begins to advance off the goal line toward an attacker. As the distance to the ball decreases, a goalkeeper should begin to break her body movement down by shifting into smaller movements known as the "cha-cha-cha." A goalkeeper is then able to maintain balance and body control. As she advances, she should never expose the near-post area, and she should be aware of the positions of teammates.

Like the dance steps of the mambo, a goalkeeper's steps should be small and smooth. As the goalkeeper is advancing to an attacker in a sprint, she will need to slow herself down. She must break these large sprint steps into much smaller, controlled steps so that she can prepare to perform a skill on the attacker. These three to four small steps are a form of the cha-cha. It helps to have your goalkeeper recite "cha-cha-cha" as she runs through a drill and breaks it down. It is one step forward that is smaller than the previous step, the next with the other foot will be smaller yet, and the third and possibly forth will bring her back to the basic stance and still position, ready to perform a skill on the attacker. This should be a smooth motion and without a hesitation in your goalkeeper's mind once she understands it.

When Is Movement Used in Goal?

There are three movements that a goalkeeper will use to move around the goal. These are lateral, forward and backward. All three movements should be done while in basic stance: on the balls of her feet, weight forward, and remaining level while changing directions (see Chapter 5). A goalkeeper should never let the play in front of her cause her to cross her feet when shuffling or cross the ball across the mouth of the goal. A goalkeeper should focus on the ball at all times and extend her arm to the nearest post to feel her position. Remind the goalkeeper to stay low when opening her hips; her height should not change (Figure 8). Do not let her pop up. Slight movement in her height as she moves along her angle will decrease her speed (Figures 8A, B).

Lateral

Lateral movements are used when the goalkeeper has time to move with the ball. The goalkeeper can stay behind the ball while in proper angle using lateral steps. These are very common movements for a goalkeeper.

Figures 8A-B. All movements (forward, lateral, backward) should be done while in basic stance, on the balls of her feet with her weight forward, remaining level while changing directions. When moving along the angle, the goalkeeper opens her hips, turns her shoulders, and points her toe back to the post. As you notice here in Figure A, the white line illustrates that the goalkeeper's head remains at the same level as she moves through the angle. The goalkeeper remains in her basic stance throughout the movement. In Figure B, you see the difference in height of the goalkeeper's head. By relaxing her body on her turn, she transitions out of her basic stance and is now standing upright. By doing this, your goalkeeper is losing seconds in the turn and is not preparing her body for the next play or skill that needs to be preformed. Make sure that your goalkeeper stays level and in her basic stance through all movements around the goal.

Forward

The forward movements are used as often as the lateral. These are used when goalkeepers need to close space or use a recovery run back to the posts or center of the goal.

Backward

A backpedal or backward movement is rarely used. This movement is used when a goalkeeper has gained some ground and the defense has since gained control of play. The goalkeeper must return to the goal without exposing a side and while staying behind the ball.

All three of these movements should be practiced so that a goalkeeper can perform a skill while using any one of these movements. Some helpful practice drills are included in Appendix A.

Zones and How to Play Them

Positioning is set in three different zones. These zones are important to a goalkeeper because they are used as a guide for how aggressive she needs to be to play a ball. Think of the circle as half of a pie broken into three zones (Figure 9). Zone 1 is the rectangle piece of the pie. This is the space from post to post on top of the circle. This is the most dangerous area in the circle. Zone 2 is the pie piece. This is from one post out on a 45-degree angle to the circle. It literally looks like a piece of pie. This area is the second-most dangerous area, and most shots come from this zone. The trapezoid down at the bottom of the pie is Zone 3. It is the least dangerous zone and a goalkeeper will rarely receive shots from this area.

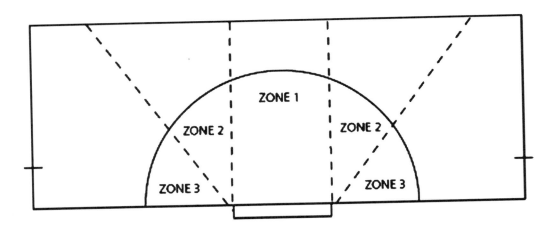

Figure 9. The 3 zones.

Zones 1 and 2 are the most dangerous, because the angle for shooting on the goal is larger. This means that Zones 1 and 2 require more aggressive action from the goalkeeper. The majority of shots will come from Zone 2, but penalty corners and other shots will create a Zone 1 shot.

All three zones are handled different ways. It is important that your goalkeeper learns and understands zones and positioning early on in her career. Just being in the correct position can prevent a goal even if your goalkeeper is uncertain of what skill to use for the situation. A goalkeeper has to make a lot of decisions within seconds to prevent the ball from going into the goal. A lot of pressure is placed on her to execute a skill when the ball is shot on goal, but correct positioning is the key to preventing unnecessary goals. Therefore, I have reviewed positioning, zones, and angles before reviewing skill sets.

Zone 1

Shots from Zone 1 need to be handled with great care. In this zone the attacker has the upper hand with the largest view of the goal. Your goalkeeper must learn to read the play and know her own ability to handle each situation, but I will attempt to give you suggestions for certain situations. Please remember that this is only a guide and not a be-all-end-all for each situation.

Each goalkeeper must learn to recognize a breakaway in Zone 1. As the attacker reaches the 25-yard line and there is no defense in sight, the goalkeeper should advance with fast-paced steps to the attacker. It is important that these steps are controlled. You do not want the goalkeeper to overrun the attacker. The goalkeeper wants to advance to cut down the angle for the attacker. As the goalkeeper advances, she should be aware of where the attacker's head is in relation to the ball. Is she looking down at the ball, oblivious to her surroundings, or is she looking up with control on the ball? If the attacker is looking down at the ball, then the goalkeeper can perform a skill and expect to win every time. I would suggest having your goalkeeper do a slide tackle (see Chapter 7) into the ball, forcing it out of the circle.

If the attacker is looking up and has complete control of the ball, have your goalkeeper shadow and stay behind the ball (between the ball and the goal) about one to two stick-lengths away from the attacker to slow her movements until help can arrive. This is very similar to what a defender would do: slow down the play and contain it until the rest of her defense can recover to help. It is important to note that in this type of aggressive play the goalkeeper should line up her body with the ball and not the attacker. These two Zone 1 situations are very similar but are handled very differently. This is often the case with goalkeeping.

Attacker with Head Down:	Attacker with Head Up:
GK quickly advances	GK quickly advances
GK performs skill	GK shadows attacker until help arrives

Table 2.

Zone 2

Zone 2 attackers are extremely dangerous. They have a bigger piece of the pie to move in, and they receive less aggressiveness from goalkeepers. A goalkeeper handling Zone 2 shots must stay poised and patient. If a goalkeeper is too aggressive in this zone, she can be beaten. Although this can happen in Zone 1, the goalkeeper is at least in the center of the field for recovery. If the goalkeeper is beaten in Zone 2, she is farther away from the center of the field and reduces her chance of recovering to the center of the goal.

As in Zone 1, your goalkeeper must learn to read the play and know her own ability to handle each situation, but I will provide some guidelines here for certain Zone 2 situations. Let me reiterate, this is only a guide and should be adapted to fit your specific situations.

If an attacker enters the circle in Zone 2, have your goalkeeper move into position so that the angle is correct. Then your goalkeeper should determine whether the attacker has her head down or has control of the ball and sight of the field in front of her. If the attacker has her head down, encourage your goalkeeper to advance as she would for a Zone 1 attacker. If the attacker has control of the ball and sight of the field, have your goalkeeper be patient by moving along her angle and watching to react to a shot. By staying along the angle and waiting for a shot, the

Attacker with Head Down:	Attacker with Head Up:
GK quickly advances	GK moves along angle
GK performs skill	GK waits for shot moving along angle
	GK reacts to shot

Table 3.

goalkeeper is increasing her opportunity to react. Most shots from Zone 2 will be toward the opposite post that the goalkeeper is moving toward, so by increasing the distance between the goalkeeper and the attacker, the goalkeeper is giving herself more chances for making a very difficult save in this situation.

Zone 3

As you can see from Table 3, Zone 3 does not have much of an angle for a shot. Most Zone 3 attackers usually bring the ball along the end line and pass it in to an attacker in Zone 2 or Zone 1. Although Zone 3 does not look dangerous, it can be. Yes, there is not much of an angle, but this should not be taken lightly. If a goalkeeper doesn't stick to the post in this angle, the ball can squeak by for a goal. A goalkeeper should not be relaxed in this area.

In Zone 3 the goalkeeper should position herself against the post closest to the ball and make sure there is no gap between her legs and the post. She should hold her ground and the post until the time is right to move or execute a skill. When making a kick, use the outside leg to ensure that there is no gap between the post and the goalkeeper. Have the goalkeeper keep her eyes on the ball and use her peripheral vision to see the rest of the field.

A Zone 3 attacker will most likely pass the ball across to Zones 1 or 2, because shots are difficult to make from Zone 3. If a pass occurs, the goalkeeper can choose to intercept it with a stick dive or follow the pass. If she follows the pass, she should open her outside hip back toward the center of the goal. Then she slides along the center of the goal and bolts out to the position of the ball to execute a skill or react to a shot.

Now that your goalkeeper understands her role and has grasped positioning and angles in the circle, we can teach her what skills she must execute to clear the ball from the circle or attacker.

chapter 5

Clearing – Maximizing Footwork and Range

The fundamentals of goalkeeping are the essence of a goalkeeper's ability to save the ball. Like field players, a goalkeeper must learn to dribble the ball, but not with a stick. She must learn to dribble with the insides of her feet, much like a soccer player would dribble a ball. She does this with her head and shoulders over the ball, weight forward, and on her toes. This helps to create kicks of equal strength in both feet. A beginning goalkeeper should start with kicking the ball from a stationary position, and then progress to kicking a moving ball, and then to kicking a ball while she is moving. While she is kicking the ball, her stick should be in her right hand, her weight forward, and she should be well-balanced, on her toes, with her knees bent.

Basic techniques must be practiced to retain their sharpness and to help keep the goalkeeper physically fit. It is essential that these skills be practiced at both low-intensity and game-like play to keep the goalkeeper sharp and ready. Being physically fit will help a goalkeeper move quickly into the right place at the right time and to use her skills to her best advantage.

Skills

The basic skills for goalkeepers are comparable to the basic skills of goalkeepers in other sports. Balance, reaction time and good judgment are keys to mastering the goal and the techniques of protecting it. Throughout this chapter you will find detailed descriptions of proper techniques and how to administer them.

Stance

Maintaining a proper stance is imperative for a goalkeeper. Without a proper stance, it is often difficult for a goalkeeper to execute her skills (Figure 10). With a proper stance, a goalkeeper should be able to move quickly in any direction and stay behind the ball. This is a crucial aspect of successful skill execution. Have your goalkeeper stand with her shoulders square to the ball, feet shoulder-width apart, and head and upper body forward (Figure 10A). She should be in a seated position. The upper torso should be slightly toward the front for balance (Figure 10B). Do not have her lean so far forward that her butt and hips are raised. A slight lean with the head over the top of her shoulders will enable her to see the ground and the action ahead of her as well. A goalkeeper should stand on the balls of her feet at all times (Figure 10C). This helps with balance and keeps the weight forward. It is extremely important that a goalkeeper keep her weight forward; therefore, maintaining this stance will ensure that the goalkeeper is doing this. Her head should be in a comfortable and steady position over the top of her knees. She should look relaxed and comfortable.

A goalkeeper should maintain from her basic stance during all techniques. During clears and angle movements, a goalkeeper's stance should be level. She should not pop up. Hips and shoulders should be at the same level through every skill and movement (Figures 8A, B).

Figure 10A.

Figure 10B.

The basic stance of the goalkeeper. In Figure C, you can see that the goalkeeper is on her toes. Her heels are off the ground, and her weight is balanced and forward.

Figure 10C.

The control box is the area in front of the feet that is close enough for a clear from the feet without much effort. Some goalkeepers refer to it as their personal space. It is about one to two square feet. It is optimal for most clears to be made inside the control box. By keeping your basic stance, this can be done with ease.

Once a goalkeeper understands proper body positioning, movement and stance, she will be well prepared to execute the various kicking techniques. Always kick through the line of body to contact the ball with as much foot as possible. Proper positioning with balanced stance permits kicking the rolling ball in one fluid motion.

Drill

Have your goalkeeper stand with her back flat against a wall. Then have her walk her feet out from the wall but keep her back flat on the wall. When she is in a seated position with her back flat against the wall, have her hold this position for two minutes. Do this three times with a rest between. Each week try to increase the time that she holds the position. This position is very close to the one she will need to have when she plays.

Clears

All of the following kicks are known as clears because the goalkeeper is clearing the ball from the goal area. All of these clears should go to the side of the field and never up the middle. Try to discourage your goalkeeper from randomly kicking the ball to the sides. Have her keep her eyes open for gaps in the field positioning or for her own player up field. This will give her more time to get back and into position before the attackers can reset and bring the ball back toward the goal. If a clear is fired up the middle, which does happen, have your goalkeeper be prepared for it to come right back at her. Most skilled attackers are prepared for rebounds like this and they anticipate that the ball is coming their way. When it does they are ready to fire it right back. This goes for the sides as well, but be especially careful of the middle (Zone 1). Most goals are scored from the middle of the field. This is a very vulnerable area for a goalkeeper. The attacker has a greater chance of getting the angle she needs to score, because she has a larger view of the goal (Figure 9).

Crossovers

Crossovers are named because of the motion that the leg must make to perform the technique. Crossovers are used for balls that are coming

Figure 11A.

Figure 11B.

Figure 11C.

Figure 11D.

Figures 11A-D. The goalkeeper starts with the majority of her weight on the kicking foot, then she drags this foot diagonally across (Figure B) and in front of her other foot, coming in contact with the ball on the instep (Figure C). She then pushes the ball across and over to the side of the body on a diagonal. She follows through with the back foot to return to the basic stance, ready for a return shot (Figure D).

Figure 11E. This figure illustrates the common mistakes that goalkeepers make with crossovers. Notice the big sweeping motion that the goalkeeper has in this technique. By sweeping in this manner, her back foot is way behind, thereby forcing her body off-balance. It will also take her much longer to get back into a basic stance position to prepare for the next attack. Notice the goalkeeper's arms. By having her blocker behind her body, she is not only pulling her weight back, but also hindering a strong kick out by not allowing her shoulders and hips to fully pivot to where she would like the ball to go. While working with your goalkeepers on crossovers, be aware of these potential mistakes and adjust your goalkeeper accordingly.

directly down the center of the stance. The goalkeeper must decide which foot to use. A crossover is usually used for slower-moving balls because it is more effective. It is also not a power clear, but more of a safety and accuracy clear.

If the ball enters down the middle but slightly to the right, the goalkeeper should use the left foot. If the ball enters down the middle but slightly to the left, the goalkeeper should use the right foot. To execute a crossover, start with the majority of the weight on the kicking foot, then drag the foot diagonally across and in front of the other foot. Come in contact with the ball on the instep of the kicking foot that is crossing over and make sure contact is inside the control box. Push the ball across and over to the side of the body on a diagonal (Figure 11). Now the goalkeeper's weight should shift to the nonkicking foot. Do not exaggerate the drag or pick up your foot in a swinging motion (Figure 11E). Big sweeping kicks are not needed and take too much time. The smaller the motion is, the faster and quicker the clear. The ball should be cleared to the side of the body, likewise to the side of the circle. By putting motion on the foot and clearing the ball as it is moving, the goalkeeper is sending the ball out at a faster rate than when it came in.

A common error is for the goalkeeper to completely miss the ball. Make sure the goalkeeper is watching the ball all the way in to the foot and concentrating on timing. In addition, the back foot should pivot to protect the goal in case the goalkeeper misses the ball. As the feet move and kick the ball to the sides, the upper body moves and pivots to the side where the ball was kicked. The hips of the goalkeeper should open and her arms and hands should point to where the ball was sent. Her knees should be bent and over the tops of her toes. Her head and shoulders should be over the tops of her knees to ensure proper balance and weight distribution (Figure 11C).

Practice is important. Start with a stationary ball and have the goalkeeper work up to kicking a ball that is in motion. When practicing have her point with her stick and glove hand to where she clears the ball. This may seem very tedious, but it will train her to open her hips and face the direction the ball went. It also ensures that she knows where she kicked the ball.

Drill

Position the goalkeeper sideways to the goal, facing you. Place a pile of balls at the 5-yard hash to the side of the goal. Send pushes to your goalkeeper's feet and have her focus on the crossover skill by sending the ball into the goal. Switch sides so that she works both feet. If the ball placement isn't appropriate for her to kick it into the goal, have her send the ball out toward the circle. You want to make sure that the goalkeeper is using the correct feet for the correct placement of the ball.

Redirects

A redirect is the technique the goalkeeper uses when she redirects the ball back out of the circle. A redirect is used for fast-paced balls that are entering to the side of the control box. If the ball enters the control box on the right, then the ball should be cleared to the right. If the ball enters the control box on the left, then the ball should be cleared to the left.

To execute a redirect, the goalkeeper must be patient and wait for the ball to come inside the control box. The goalkeeper should position the kicking foot on an angle away from the body and push the ball diagonally to the side of the body (Figures 12A, B). The goalkeeper should open her hips and position her head and shoulders over her kicking foot. All of her weight should begin on the nonkicking foot and end on the kicking foot. This helps to put more force on the ball when the kicking foot makes contact.

As when executing the crossover, the goalkeeper should point her hands and turn her shoulders to where the ball was directed. She should be in a low-seated position. Make sure that the goalkeeper is on her toes and all weight is forward. The ball should be cleared to the sides of the circle (Figure 12C). These clears, however, should be big and travel completely

Figure 12A.

Figure 12B.

Figure 12C.

Figures 12A-C. The goalkeeper positions
the kicking foot on an angle out and away
from her body (Figure B) and pushes the
ball diagonally to the side of her body.
The goalkeeper opens her hips and
positions her head and shoulders over her
kicking foot. The foot should only move
about one to two inches forward and to
the side. The ball hits the instep of the
foot, and the goalkeeper follows through
by bringing the nonkicking foot level with
the kicking foot thereby returning to a
basic stance ready for a return shot
(Figure C).

outside the circle. As with the crossover, the goalkeeper can send the ball out of the circle at a faster rate than it came in. With redirects, however, only a little motion is needed because the ball will be entering at a faster rate than a crossover ball. Therefore, the foot should only move about one to two inches forward and to the side. The ball should hit the instep of the foot to exit the control box correctly (Figure 12B). Remember, the goalkeeper must be in her basic stance. Redirects are widely used today and are most effective because the ball travels out of the control box in a controlled, quick pace.

Drill

Position your goalkeeper sideways to the goal, facing you. Place a pile of balls at the 5-yard hash to the side of the goal. Send pushes to your goalkeeper's feet and have her focus on the redirect skill by sending the ball into the goal. Switch sides so that she works both feet. If the ball placement isn't appropriate, have the goalkeeper send the ball out toward the circle. You want to make sure she is using the correct feet for the correct placement of the ball.

Toe Clears

A toe clear is a clear used with the tips of the toes. It is used to place force and urgency on the ball. When using a toe clear, however, a goalkeeper cannot control the ball. To execute this skill, have the goalkeeper place her nonkicking foot next to but slightly behind the ball. She should

Figure 13A.

Figure 13B.

Figures 13A-B. The goalkeeper places her nonkicking foot next to but slightly behind the ball. She then swings her kicking foot through, almost dragging the foot on the ground, and contacts the ball with her toes (Figure A). As she comes through with the kick, she bends her knee, thrusting her foot upward, and places a little hop in the kick for more power (Figure B). Then she brings the leg back down to meet the other leg in a basic stance ready for the next shot.

then swing her kicking foot through, almost dragging the foot on the ground, and contact the ball with her toes (Figure 13). The ball should hit when her toes are under her equipment. The knee of her kicking foot should be bent when she comes in contact with the ball, to create more power. As she comes through the kick, she should place a little hop in the kick to generate even more power. As a follow-through, she should thrust the kicking foot leg upward and then bring it back down to meet the other leg in set position ready for the next shot (Figure 13B). For loose balls that are just outside the control box, have the goalkeeper pull the ball into the control box with her stick.

Drill

Line up some balls at the 3-yard line and have your goalkeeper kick each one into the goal with her right foot. Then line up the balls again and have her do the same with her left foot. Another version of this drill is to have your goalkeeper run from a designated area, set up for a kick into the goal, return to the designated area and then back to the balls for a kick.

Punch Clears

A punch clear is used when the ball is just a little bit out of a goalkeeper's reach or for a 50/50 ball. It is a skill used to tackle the ball away from the attacker and for clearing a ball out of the circle. In other words, the ball is slightly off the attacker's stick and the goalkeeper knows that she cannot get to the ball quickly enough on her feet.

This skill looks like a baseball player's slide into second base. To use it a goalkeeper must have good distance and speed judgment. She has to know her body's limitations and know her attacker. She must advance quickly and prepare herself in pre-tackle position to time the clear. She should be about a foot away from the ball when she begins her slide. The non-kicking foot kicks back and tucks behind the butt. The kicking leg, still bent at the knee, contacts the ball while the goalkeeper is moving through the slide. The bottom of her foot contacts the ball. Her kicking leg is still bent, and when she comes in contact with the ball, she should push her leg into full extension (Figures 14A-C). This is for extra "umph" and direction on the ball.

The ankle of the kicking foot should hit the ground first, followed by the rest of the leg and side of the kicking foot. She should allow her body to fall to the ground on the side of the punch leg. The goalkeeper should land mainly on her buttocks and forearm, with her weight back and on the side of the kicking foot. The nonkicking leg is tucked and used as a guard for a deflection, while her glove hand is up and ready for a flick. Her stick hand should be out on the ground ready for a deflection as

Figure 14A.

Figure 14B.

Figure 14C.

Figure 14D.

Figure 14E.

Figures 14A-E. The goalkeeper tucks her nonkicking foot back and bends her kicking knee as she is coming down into a slide (Figure A). She contacts the ball with the bottom of her foot (Figure B) and pushes her kicking leg into a full extension (Figure C). Once the clear has been made, the goalkeeper gets up quickly by pushing up with her glove hand and stick while scissoring her legs together (Figure D). As she gets up, her weight should shift forward, and all the momentum should be forward toward where the ball was cleared (Figure E).

well. Her head should immediately be in line with the ball and ready to recover (Figure 14C). By this positioning, she can cover a lot of area and be prepared for a return shot. Punch clears are like toe clears; they cannot be used for direction or control.

Please note that this is the only clear where the goalkeeper's weight is toward the back. Once the clear has been made, the goalkeeper will need to know how to get up and return to a set position. Because the goalkeeper's weight is back, the first thing she must do is push her chest and head forward. She will need to put her glove hand between her legs and push up. At the same time, she will be pushing up with her stick hand. Her kicking foot is simultaneously pushing up with her heel as it tucks to the chest. The nonkicking leg is also pushing and tucking into the chest (Figure 14D). As she gets up, her weight and momentum should shift forward. Once everything is tucked and pushing upward, the goalkeeper can continue pushing up through the base into her basic stance (Figure 14E). Make sure the goalkeeper is keeping her weight forward and she is recovering on angle to where the ball was cleared.

Drill

Have the goalkeeper sit in the punch clear position, with her leg cocked back and her knee into her chest. She should place her front foot on its side (Figure 14B). Have a pile of balls on hand. Place a ball, one at a time, in the arch of the foot and have your goalkeeper push her leg forward and out, extending her leg and knee (Figure 14C). This will send the ball forward. Have your goalkeeper work on speed and strength from this position. Be sure to work both feet. When she is comfortable with this position, you will need to teach her how to get into this position. Use the track field's sand pit at your school to practice sliding and punch clearing using both feet. When she is comfortable with this drill, you can have her perform live punch clears on grass. Start with some stationary balls that she can run to and punch out to get the timing. Then advance to rolling balls. The last step is to practice this skill with attackers. Overpass a ball to an attacker and have both the goalkeeper and the attacker try to intercept it.

chapter 6

Diving into Saves

There are four basic saves to execute when a kicking clear is not an option: glove saves, stick saves, lunge saves and split saves.

Glove Save

A glove save is used when the ball is in the air and cannot be stopped by the legs or feet. For beginners, a glove save is often a reactionary save: the ball is coming toward the goalkeeper's head and her reaction is to stop it. After training, the goalkeeper will be able to stop the ball and direct it into the control box for a basic kicking clear out of the danger zone.

In a glove save the goalkeeper's entire body should be behind the ball in case the ball spins behind her hand. The goalkeeper should square up with the ball and not the attacker. She should follow the ball into her glove and allow her body to move with the impact so the ball won't propel forward. She can then guide the ball to her feet (Figures 15 A-C). Once this is done a basic clear can be administered. Have the goalkeeper take caution not to propel the ball forward when the ball enters the glove. A skilled goalkeeper will force the ball out and in front of her without propelling it, but a novice will often get a touch on it and change its direction by propelling. Have the beginning goalkeeper start by catching the ball and dropping it to her feet. (There are special gloves she can use for this training.) This should be done with light tosses. If she isn't using a glove, use tennis balls to start training. The goalkeeper should catch the ball in front of her chest with her fingers pointed up, then slowly turn her wrist clockwise and drop the ball when her fingers are pointing down toward her feet (Figures 15A-C). When the ball is at her feet, she can clear the ball. As the reaction time and movement becomes understood, have the goalkeeper put on the appropriate glove and try it. After that is learned, speed up your tosses and then graduate to sending flicks via a stick.

Figure 15A.

Figure 15B.

Figures 15A-C. The goalkeeper follows the ball into her glove and allows her arm to give with the impact (Figure A). Her fingers are pointed up, and she slowly turns her wrist clockwise, guiding the ball to her feet (Figure B). The ball drops when her fingers are pointing down toward her feet, and she prepares her body to make a clear (Figure C).

Figure 15C.

Sometimes goalkeepers don't get the perfect ball to send to their feet to clear out. Often times the ball is moving very fast and goalkeepers just have enough time to clear it out of the way of the goalmouth. As the ball is entering the glove, the goalkeeper turns her wrist and forearm to the side to guide the ball to the side of the goal. Make sure that your goalkeeper is still staying behind the ball and that she is keeping her hand firm (Figures 16A, B). In addition, when your goalkeeper makes this motion, she cannot extend her elbow to straighten her arm. A straight arm is considered propelling the ball. It is also important to note that the goalkeeper should stay square and not move her shoulders. In Figure 16A, you see that the goalkeeper is slightly turned; by doing this she has exposed the goal. Her body should be square and behind the ball and the ball should only be guided to the sides with her arm, wrist and glove.

Drill

Start with some tennis balls and tennis racquet. Using the tennis racquet, hit the tennis balls to the goalkeeper. Have her try to send the balls to her feet or out to the sides of her body using her glove only. Work both sides of the body.

Stick Save

A stick save is for balls that are above the leg guard and cannot be reached by leg or glove. As with the glove save, a goalkeeper using a stick save should never swing or propel the ball. The key is to always position the goalkeeper so that her hands, stick, eyes, head and chest are behind the ball. She should absorb the ball and bunt it to the ground in her control box so that she can use a kicking clear to get the ball out of the danger area (Figures 17A, B). The objective is to concentrate on coordination control. As the ball comes toward the goalkeeper, she should position her body behind the ball, watching the ball all the way to her stick. When the ball hits the stick, the goalkeeper should force the ball down to the ground. She should see where the ball is at all times and where she sent the ball after she made the save. Her body is behind the ball so that it does not spin behind her, or in case she misses the ball with her stick. Start as you do with glove saves. Send light tosses toward the goalkeeper and have her position her body behind the ball and bunt the ball with her stick to the ground. This takes more coordination, concentration and timing than the glove save, so more practice may be needed on this skill. As the goalkeeper advances, graduate to sending flicks via a stick.

Like the glove save, goalkeepers can also force the ball to the side of their body and goal. Oftentimes the ball is slightly beyond the reach of

Figure 16A.

Figure 16B.

Figures 16A-B. *The goalkeeper follows the ball into her glove with her fingers pointed up. When the ball makes contact, she turns her arm and wrist and forces or guides the ball to the side of the goal. Notice that she does not extend her elbow. This applies to both sides of the body. As you notice here, the goalkeeper has her body turned a little as she forces the ball to the side. The goal would be better protected if she were square to the ball and not opening her hips and shoulders to expose the goal. This movement should really only be done with the hand, wrist and arm.*

Figure 17A.

Figure 17B.

Figures 17A-B. The goalkeeper follows the ball into her stick. She bats the ball down and guides it to her feet (Figure A). Notice that the goalkeeper keeps the stick firm and does not swing at the ball. As the ball is on its way down to her feet, she prepares her body to make a clear (Figure B).

Figure 18. When the ball contacts the stick, the goalkeeper has a firm grip on the stick and forces the ball to the side of the goal. As you notice here, the goalkeeper has her body turned a little as she forces the ball to the side. I would prefer her to be square to the ball and not opening her hips and shoulders to expose the goal. This movement should only be done with the arm and stick.

the goalkeeper so the stick does become a handy extension of the arm. By reaching out for the ball, the goalkeeper can make contact with it, and with a slight bunt (being careful not to swing the stick) the goalkeeper can force the ball to the side of the goal (Figure 18). Remember to have your goalkeeper follow the ball and prepare for a return shot.

Drill

Start with some tennis balls and a tennis racquet. Using the racquet, hit tennis balls to the goalkeeper. Have her try to send the ball to her feet or out to the stick side of her body, using her stick only. Work only the stick side of the body.

Over-the-Head Aerials

Occasionally a skilled attacker will send a flick over the goalkeeper's head so that it drops into the goal. Your goalkeeper, however, can touch this ball and send it over the top of the goal. the move is very similar to what you would see a soccer goalkeeper do for aerials. Have your goalkeeper start in a stationary position then work up to a backpedal, turn

Figure 19. In this figure the goalkeeper is on her way up, trying to catch the ball in the air and force it over the goal behind her. Notice the arch in the back and both hands up reaching for the ball.

and sprint. Your goalkeeper must jump upward, arching her back and pushing her arms over the top of the goal (Figure 19). First have your goalkeeper practice this motion without a ball. It is a very awkward motion. Next use a large ball such as a soccer ball to get the timing down. Gradually work your way up to the field hockey ball. This skill is extremely difficult because of the timing of the jump with different heights and ball speeds. Practice different scenarios with your goalkeeper.

Stick Dives

For balls that are beyond the reach of the goalkeeper or that are too wide for a split, a stick dive is used. The concept for the stick dive is the same as for the basic stick save, except that the goalkeeper is diving in the air or along the ground. The stick becomes an extension of the arm for blocking and saving balls.

From her basic stance, a goalkeeper should position her feet and knees facing front and her arms to her sides. She then takes a step with the foot nearest the ball and leaps into a dive to save the ball. This leap can be a slide along the ground or a leap into the air. She should transfer her body weight to her fully flexed leg nearest the ball, then push off into a dive. The momentum will force the other leg and arm to follow the rest of the body. She reaches for the ball by extending her stick and arm with the palms of her hands facing the ball. Her head and shoulders should extend toward the ball (Figures 20A, B). As in other skills, a goalkeeper should always position her head and chest behind the ball. It is crucial that the head remain as close as possible to the line of the ball. A goalkeeper should contact the ground on her side and not on her stomach. Her outer thigh should hit the ground first, followed by her hip, rib cage and shoulders. Once she is on the ground she may roll to her stomach to get up. Her head is now between her arms, eyes focused on the ball.

Sometimes a stick dive is used as a last effort in a scramble, and the goalkeeper is out of position or knows she is going to get beaten. The goalkeeper must scramble to clear the ball out of the danger zone. Often times in a dive, the goalkeeper has no control as to where the ball will be redirected. That's why focus and following the ball's movement are important. A goalkeeper should try to keep the ball in front of her for protection, but being on the ground after the dive creates vulnerability. Therefore, a goalkeeper will use a stick save often while down on the ground. Make sure the goalkeeper does not swing at the ball. Her arms should stay parallel, and any stick movement should be used with the wrist only. Once the goalkeeper is on the ground, she cannot smother or cover the ball. The ball must be seen and easily accessed on the ground. The only thing a goalkeeper can do in this situation is be a strong wall. She must lay there with arms and legs extended in front of her, prepared for a flick and ready to react. Her defense should come to her aid to help her clear the ball from the danger zone. Her only form of defense when she is in a vulnerable environment like this is her stick. She can trap the ball with her stick and try to hold it in front of her until her defense comes to help. She should keep her wrist firm and angle the stick to block. Once the ball is cleared, the goalkeeper can get up and prepare for the next attack.

As your goalkeeper gets off the ground and back into position, have her focus on the ball. While still watching the ball, she should turn into a push-up position. From here she needs to pull her knees to her chest, tuck them underneath her body and fully push herself up like a push-up. As her legs come up under her (Figures 20C, D) she needs to keep all momentum going forward toward the ball. The goalkeeper should try this very slowly at first until she gets the hang of it, then do it at a quick

Figure 20A.

Figure 20B.

Figures 20A-B. The goalkeeper dives to save the ball (Figure A). She extends her stick and arm, with her palms facing the ball. She contacts the ground on her side (Figure B), with her eyes focused on the ball.

Figure 20C.

Figure 20D.

Figures 20C-D. Next she pushes up with her arms using the glove hand and knuckles of the stick hand, then pulls her knees to her chest and underneath her body (Figure C). While pushing up with her arms, she turns her body, puts the top leg over and fully pushes herself up to her feet in the direction of the ball.

pace. Work some drills into your practice that have your goalkeeper on her stomach and getting up to play a ball.

Drill

With your goalkeeper kneeling, lob a soccer ball to either side of her body. Have your goalkeeper reach out for the ball and stop it. Make sure the tosses are just slightly out of her reach so that she has to dive to either side to get the ball. Gradually work toward using a field hockey ball. If your goalkeeper is scared to dive, try using mats on either side of her or practicing in the sand until she feels comfortable enough to use the skill on the field. Once your goalkeeper grasps the concept, have her stand in a "safety crouch." This is an exaggerated basic stance in which her heels almost touching her behind. Once she is able to perform the skills from this position, have her stand in her basic stance. Concentrate on certain heights and levels of the ball first. Once the goalkeeper has mastered each, you can do random tosses. After tosses you should graduate to using a stick and ball. Note that diving is very tiring and can cause wear and tear on your goalkeeper. Be aware of the time you are spending on this skill set and make sure you place some breaks between skill set practices.

Lunge Save

A lunge save is another reflex save that the goalkeeper uses when the ball is moving too quickly and is just a bit out of her reach. To execute this skill she stretches her leg and foot out by lunging to where the ball is heading. She transfers her body weight from her nonlunge leg onto the lunge leg. Her hip should be opened wide, and her foot should be pointed to where the ball needs to be redirected. Her lunge leg is placed in the direct line of the ball. Her head and shoulders must be over her lunge knee and the lunge knee should be bent. The inside of her leg should be facing the ball, and the ball should contact the inside of the saving foot, slightly to the front of the body. The technique is completed by pushing the lunge foot into the upright position as fast as possible (Figure 21A-D). She then should return to a ready position and face the direction of the ball. If the ball is in the air, hits a goalkeeper's leg guards and drops to the ground, the goalkeeper must use a kicking clear to direct the ball out of the circle. To practice, start with slow balls that are slightly out of reach of the goalkeeper and then graduate to fast-paced balls. Vary the heights on these balls (on the ground and slightly off the ground).

Figure 21A.

Figure 21B.

Figure 21C.

Figure 21D.

Figures 21A-D. The goalkeeper lunges to where the ball is heading. Her weight transfers, her hips open wide, and her foot points to where the ball needs to be redirected (Figure B). Her head and shoulders are over her bent lunge knee. The ball contacts the instep of the foot, and the goalkeeper follows through by bringing her feet in line with each other (Figure C), returning to her basic stance (Figure D).

When a ball is just a foot or two off the ground, a goalkeeper can use the save concept of the lunge save. These are very difficult balls to defend because they are too low for a stick or reverse stick dive to get down in time. The goalkeeper is forced into a lunge to save these.

Drill

Have your goalkeeper stand on a line and step into a lunge with her right leg along the line. Make sure she has good form and is reaching far into the lunge. The foot should be angled back so the ball can be reflected out on an angle instead of flat or back at the attacker. After your goalkeeper has practiced this a few times working both legs, then start sending her a few balls to either side. Make sure the ball is not just hitting the foot, but is meeting the ball and sending it back out.

Split Save

A split save is a technique used to stop a ball that is too wide for a lunge save — in other words, when the goalkeeper needs to cover as much area of the goal as possible in very little time. A split save is usually used for hard, quick-paced shots that are sent to the corners of the goal.

To execute this save, have the goalkeeper keep her eyes on the ball while in the basic stance. The goalkeeper must get her head as close as possible to the flight of the ball. She should transfer her weight from the nonkicking leg to the kicking leg and explode out of her basic stance toward the path of the ball. Both feet should leave the ground. Her kicking foot's toes should be pointed to the sky, with her leg fully extended. The goalkeeper should bring her head over her kicking knee by stretching out both arms over the kicking leg. One hand should go behind the leg and the other in front. If splitting to the right, the stick hand should move behind the split leg and beyond the knee. Place the stick behind the right leg to extend the reach, while the glove hand is in front of the knee ready for a return aerial shot (Figure 22A, B). If splitting to the left, the glove hand should extend behind the knee of the splitting leg to be used as an extension of the knee to increase the height of the pad. The stick hand should rest in front of the splitting leg and be used as an extended blocker. By pulling the head and hands over the kicking foot knee, the goalkeeper automatically turns her shoulders and upper body and allows contact with the ball to be on a lateral plane. The goalkeeper should contact the ball with the inside of the kicking foot. Her nonkicking leg should follow, dragging behind in a tucked position. The calf muscle of the kicking foot should hit the ground first. Be sure to keep the foot parallel to the ground, with the toes pointed to the sky. The goalkeeper

Figure 22A.

Figure 22B.

Figures 22A-B. The goalkeeper explodes out of her basic stance toward the ball. Her toes are pointed to the sky, and her leg is fully extended. She places her head over her knee and stretches out both arms (Figure A). In this figure, she is splitting to the right, so the stick hand moves behind the split le, while the glove hand is in front of the knee. Her nonkicking leg follows, dragging behind in a hurdle position (Figure B).

Figures 22C-D. To get up, the goalkeeper places one hand behind the hip and the other hand in front of the hip and pushes up. At the same time, she digs her back toe into the ground, pulls her legs together, and tucks them underneath her to help push herself to an upright position.

Figure 22E.

She is now on her feet and returned to her basic stance, prepared for another attack.

should fall into a hurdle or seated position. When the goalkeeper contacts the ground, she should keep herself prepared for a return shot. For this reason the arms are extended over the knee and the nonkicking leg is tucked like a blocker behind the goalkeeper (Figure 22B). When the first shot is deflected, the goalkeeper should recover as quickly as possible to her basic stance.

Split saves are used for balls on the ground that are out of reach and for balls slightly in the air that are out of reach. When a ball is just a foot or two off the ground, a goalkeeper can use the save concept of the split save. These are very difficult balls to defend because they are too low for a stick or reverse stick dive to get down in time. The goalkeeper is forced into a split to save these.

To return to the basic stance position, have the goalkeeper place one hand behind her hip, the other hand in front of her hip and push up (Figure 22C). She should dig the toe of her back foot into the ground, pull her legs together, and tuck her legs underneath her to help push herself to an upright position. The legs should push up and pull together in a scissor-like position underneath the body (Figure 22D). Remember that the goalkeeper should keep all momentum moving forward and her eyes focused on the ball (Figure 22E). Momentum helps with recovering into a ready position, so as soon as the goalkeeper hits the ground, she should immediately start to push herself up toward the direction of the deflected ball.

Drill

Have your goalkeeper start in a safety crouch with a stationary ball. Have her extend her leg into a split toward the stationary ball. When she is comfortable with this, she can begin from her basic stance. Next, place a pile of balls at the stroke mark and have your goalkeeper stand on one post. Send a few balls to the far post so that they are out of foot reach of the goalkeeper. Have your goalkeeper split to retrieve them. Make sure that her head and hands are coming through in the split and that she is gaining distance. Work both sides so that your goalkeeper can be adept at splitting equally on both sides. Vary this drill by having the goalkeeper face out toward the side line as if the ball were coming from this position and being passed to you at the stroke mark. When you are ready, yell "Go" and send the ball to the opposite side of the goal. The goalkeeper must turn and split to retrieve the ball.

chapter 7

Specialty Skills – Setting up for the Next Level

This chapter is comprised of four specialty skills. There are others, but in this book I am only introducing four main techniques.

Block Tackle

A block tackle is a specialty skill reserved for goalkeepers who have perfected their basic stance, angles, clears and dives. A block tackle is a very reliable and versatile skill. It is widely used for one-on-one situations, but it can also be used for corners, hard drives into the circle and penalty strokes. A goalkeeper should be able to block tackle on both sides of the body; however, most goalkeepers use their right side to maximize the use of the glove and stick. By using this skill, the goalkeeper is then able to cover more of the goal. The majority of goalkeepers will not be able to outrun an oncoming attacker, so learning when and how to execute a block tackle is an essential specialty skill for every intermediate goalkeeper. A block tackle can be used in any zone, however, it is best used when the ball is in Zone 1 or 2 (see Chapter 4).

The goalkeeper should stand relaxed and in her basic stance. As the attacker advances toward the top of the circle, the goalkeeper should charge in a controlled manner toward the ball and the attacker. The goalkeeper should only execute the block tackle when she is a few feet away from the attacker, and the attacker is able to drive the ball in the goal. I tell my goalkeepers that they must be a stick-length or more away from the attacker. If your goalkeeper advances when the attacker is closer than a stick-length away, she will not have time to execute the skill, and she will obstruct her view of the ball.

When the attacker's stick is pulled back and coming down toward the ball in a downswing, the goalkeeper needs to execute the block tackle. A trained goalkeeper will see the stick move back and start to come through for a hit. She should position her body directly between the ball and the

Figure 23. The goalkeeper swings her legs underneath her body and lands on her side in a tucked position. Notice here that her legs are curled up and her knees are tucked to her chest. Her head is positioned almost over the top of her knees. She is resting on her elbow which is tucked in tight to her torso. The glove hand is prepared for a flick shot.

net. She should then swing her legs underneath her body, land on the side of her buttock and thigh, and roll down to land on her ribs and lower arm. One leg should be resting on the other, with the knees pulled up toward the chest (Figure 23).

All this is done in one quick motion. The goalkeeper is now a wall between the ball and the goal. She should be on the ground in a tucked position. Her legs should be curled up and her knees tucked to her chest. Her upper body should be upright protecting the aerial space, with her head positioned almost over the top of her knees so that she can see the ball if it hits her pads. She should be resting on her elbow for balance, and it should be tucked in tight to her torso (Figure 23). The other hand is for protection in case the attacker executes a flick over the goalkeeper's legs. The goalkeeper's hope is that the ball will be deflected slightly away from the attacker so that her defense can help while she is on the ground. If the ball is knocked back to the attacker and the attacker proceeds to drive it again, the goalkeeper must stay in the position and try to block the ball. She should not attempt to get up unless there is some defense around her or unless the attacker is far enough away. If the ball is bouncing, the goalkeeper can tap it down to the ground, but she must quickly uncover it. A goalkeeper cannot lie on the ball or cover it up. Also, she can use her stick to free a ball that is stuck in her pads. An attempt to clear the stuck ball from equipment should be made if this occurs. If the ball is caught in front of the goalkeeper, she should call her defense to help her escort the ball out of the danger zone. If there is no defense to help, the goalkeeper must try to spin on her buttocks and hit the ball with her stick, sweeping it out of play, or try to stand up with her feet behind the ball and execute a clear.

Return Position

If the ball is deflected out in front of the goalkeeper, she will need to get up and follow through. All her weight should be going forward, and her eyes should be focused on the ball. From this position, the goalkeeper must pull the top leg over the bottom leg, place the foot flat on the ground and push up and forward with the forearm and glove hand. Her bottom should push off the ground at the same time as her forearm and tuck and turn so that the foot becomes flat on the ground. Have the goalkeeper step into her stance from here.

What if the Ball Gets Behind the Goalkeeper?

If the attacker tries to dribble around the goalkeeper, a slight extension of the legs or arms will lengthen the goalkeeper's ability to block the goal and possibly slow down the play. If the ball has passed the goalkeeper, she should quickly get up as described above, with all of her momentum forward. The goalkeeper then needs to turn, quickly recover to the center of the goal and square out to where the ball is on the field. In a last ditch attempt to save the ball, a stick dive back to the near post can be executed. Oftentimes on this stick dive back, goalkeepers will dive onto their stomachs. Please be careful of this and make sure your goalkeeper is still executing the proper skills and techniques even in a hurried, last-effort situation.

Drill

Have your goalkeeper stand on the goal line and sprint to the stroke mark with breakdown steps. A feeder will be standing on the 10-yard line with a pile of balls. When the goalkeeper breaks down, pull back and come through with a strong hit. The goalkeeper should practice watching the stick movement and then dropping into a block tackle when the stick is coming down into a hit. As your goalkeeper becomes more advanced, change the types of hits (flicks, chips, etc.) so that the goalkeeper can see the difference in each coming off the stick. Eventually advance to live play.

This is very tiring, and it can cause wear and tear on your goalkeeper. Be aware of the time that you are spending on this skill set and make sure you place some breaks during the skill set practice.

Slide Tackle

A slide tackle has the same concept as a block tackle, but the goalkeeper is sliding into the ball. It is executed the same way and with the same positioning as the block tackle, but the goalkeeper is in motion and slides through the ball and the attacker. This forces the attacker over the goalkeeper and the ball out and in front of the goalkeeper. This skill can be used in any zone in the circle; however, it is only recommended for Zones 1 and 2 (see Chapter 4).

Please note that the goalkeeper is forcing an attacker over top of her, and if this skill is not done correctly, someone can get hurt. The proper gear is essential. If you are teaching this to a goalkeeper with live attackers, it may be best to warn your attackers to prepare to jump during training for their safety. In addition, make sure your goalkeeper has a properly fitting helmet. These are the types of situations where helmets can be kicked or pulled off of a goalkeeper.

The goalkeeper should be one to two stick-lengths away to perform this skill. This skill is used when the goalkeeper is closer to the attacker and charging at her. The goalkeeper charges in a controlled forward movement to the attacker. She then swings her legs underneath her body, lands on the side of her buttock and thigh, and rolls down to land on her ribs and lower arm. All of this is done in one quick motion, sliding on her side through and into the ball. The goalkeeper should be on the ground in a tucked position. Her legs should be curled up, with one leg over the top of the other and her knees tucked to her chest. Her upper body should be upright, with her head positioned almost over the top of her knees. She should land on her elbow, and her arm and stick should be fully extended (Figure 24A). Once this skill is executed, the goalkeeper should quickly get up and prepare for a rebound shot.

Return Position

If this skill is executed and timed correctly, the ball will be deflected out and in front of the goalkeeper. All of her weight should be going forward, and her eyes should be focused on the ball. From this position, the goalkeeper will need to pull the top leg over the bottom leg, place the foot flat on the ground (Figures 24B, C) and push up and forward with the forearm. The bottom leg must push off the ground at the same

Figure 24A.

Figure 24B.

Figure 24C.

Figures 24A-C. The goalkeeper advances toward the ball and swings her legs underneath her body. She lands on her side, sliding through and into the ball (Figure A). Notice here that the goalkeeper is in a tucked position, much like the block tackle. To get up, the goalkeeper puts her top leg over the bottom and pushes up with both hands, keeping her eyes focused on the ball (Figure B). As she pushes up, she keeps all of her weight going forward (Figure C).

time as the forearm and tuck and turn so that the foot becomes flat on the ground. Have the goalkeeper step into her stance from here.

What if the Ball Gets Behind the Goalkeeper?

If the ball has passed the goalkeeper, she must quickly get up as described above, with all of her momentum forward. The goalkeeper then needs to turn, quickly recover to the center of the goal and square out to where the ball is on the field. In a last-ditch attempt to save the ball, a stick dive back to the near post can be executed. As I mentioned in the section on block tackles, it is important that your goalkeeper is still executing the proper skills and techniques even in these kinds of situations.

Drills

Place five cones about five yards apart on diagonal angles from each other (Figure 25). At the top cone place a live attacker with a ball. Have your goalkeeper run up to each cone and slide tackle into it. If it is done right, she should be sliding through the cone. Since they are on angles, your goalkeeper should be slide tackling on both sides of her body. Make sure she is tackling the cone and getting up as quickly as possible to run to the next cone. After tackling the last cone, the goalkeeper will have a live ball and attacker to tackle. Have your dummy attacker dribble forward, with her head down and no vision of the field. After your goalkeeper has tackled the dummy attacker, your goalkeeper should recover and run back toward the beginning of the drill and stick dive. Start by emphasizing proper tech-

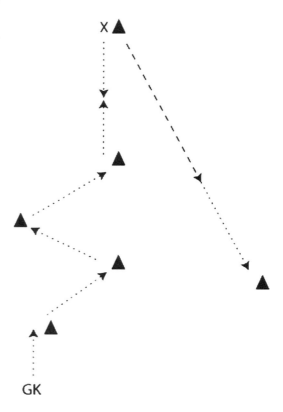

Figure 25. Place the cones about five to seven yards apart. At the top place a live attacker with a ball. Have your goalkeeper sprint and slide tackle into each cone using both sides of the body. After tackling the last cone, the goalkeeper will have a live attacker with a ball to tackle. A variation of this drill is to have the goalkeeper recover after the live tackle, turn and sprint to the last cone on the diagonal, then stick dive. You can have this stick dive be stationary or with a live ball.

nique and move through the drill slowly. Work up to having this drill timed. A variation of this drill would be to add a live ball for the stick dive back to goal or to have the attacker play true.

This is a very tiring drill, and it can cause wear and tear on your goalkeeper. Be aware of the time that you are spending on this skill set and make sure that you place some breaks during the skill set practice.

Penalty Stroke

A penalty stroke is awarded when the defense commits a foul in the circle that prevents a probable goal. For instance, if the goalkeeper were to cover the ball, a penalty stroke would be called. In addition, a penalty stroke is also used in tournaments to determine the winner if the score is still tied after overtime. The ball is placed seven yards in front of the center of the goal line at the stroke mark. The attacker chooses to push, flick or scoop the ball into the goal with a few steps and one touch of the ball. The goalkeeper must have her feet on the goal line and may not move until the ball is played. This places the attacker in a very strong position and the goalkeeper in a weak one — the rule intends to do that. The attacker usually disguises her intentions to gain an extra advantage. If she has sufficient strength in her arms, she may not need to take the playing distance steps that are allowed, which, though they increase her power on the ball, gives the goalkeeper a small chance to guess the direction of it. The attacker needs to add power to the ball by using a strong thrust from her back foot to propel her body weight into the ball. This shift produces power through the trunk of the body and adds a quick movement of the arms to lift or spin the ball toward the goal. The shots that are most likely to defeat a goalkeeper are those that are fast-paced and directed to the extreme corners of the goal. The attacker will vary the height and direction of the shot, preying on the weakness of the goalkeeper.

To defend a penalty stroke, a goalkeeper should take her time when preparing her stance and mental focus on the ball. Have the goalkeeper take a deep breath to instill calmness and concentration. She should be determined to come out successful. One thing I must stress is that the goalkeeper always tries to stop the ball with her hands. Positioning is different for each individual goalkeeper. It's a matter of comfort. However, for the purposes of this book, I will be showing one way to defend a penalty stroke. As the goalkeeper becomes more familiar with her skills, let her experiment and find her own creativity for this skill.

The goalkeeper should position herself with her feet and knees facing front (Figure 26 A). Since the goalkeeper has to have her feet on the goal line, have her place the back part of her heels on the line (Figure 26 B). This increases distance and reaction time, but it also decreases the chance of the ball rolling over the goal line. This also goes along with the angle theory. By positioning the goalkeeper closer to the ball in a stroke, the goalkeeper narrows the angle for shooting as much as possible. The goalkeeper should be in the center of the goal with her feet shoulder-width apart. She should be in a crouched seated position that is lower than her normal basic stance. This lower center of gravity will make it easier for the goalkeeper to move upward and downward. Her hands should be extended out and to her sides (Figure 26A). The stick should be held in the usual position, 1/3 down the shaft (Figure 26A). With this positioning the goalkeeper looks bigger, as if she can reach all points of the goal. She is now poised to move aggressively in any direction. Once the ball is sent toward the goal, the goalkeeper has to react to the ball. The goalkeeper should watch the ball, evaluate its flight path and commit to the save. The goalkeeper should always move her head and hands first for all penalty strokes. Her legs may be longer but her hands are quicker.

To succeed at a penalty stroke, the goalkeeper must have her head and body in position behind the ball to execute a solid block and safely redirect the ball. It is crucial that her head remain as close as possible to the line of the ball. Her arms should remain extended and out at her sides as she steps with the foot nearest the direction of the ball. The goalkeeper transfers her body weight over the fully flexed leg nearest the ball and pushes off with her foot to begin a head-first dive toward the ball (Figure 27A). The momentum of the body will bring the opposite leg with the body. The extended stick, glove hand, head and shoulders should now be in the air toward the ball. When at all possible, try to have the goalkeeper place her head behind the ball and the palms of her hands facing the ball. The goalkeeper should be able to see the ball make contact with her glove or stick. She then should contact the ground on her side and not her stomach (Figure 27B). By placing her entire body behind the ball, she ensures that it will not roll or bounce behind her once she makes the block.

The landing of this skill is just as important as the save itself. When the goalkeeper is in the air, her arms are extended and reaching for the ball for the save (Figure 27A). After the save has been executed, the goalkeeper should then pull her arms in and tuck them into her chest, rolling her shoulders in and forward (Figure 27B). When the goalkeeper lands

Figure 26A.

Figures 26A-B. The goalkeeper is positioned with her feet and knees facing front, shoulder-width apart, in the center of the goal (Figure A). She has her heels on the goal line (Figure B). In this figure, I would prefer the goalkeeper to be in a lower position, but as I mentioned earlier, it is about the comfort of the goalkeeper.

Figure 26B.

Figure 27A.

Figure 27B.

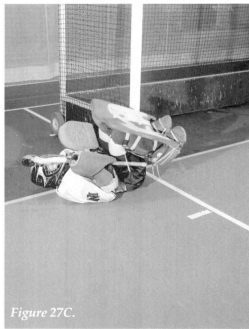

Figure 27C.

Figures 27A-C. The goalkeeper pushes off into a head-first dive toward the ball. Her extended stick, glove hand, head and shoulders are bounding in the air toward the ball. Notice that the goalkeeper's palms are facing the ball. After saving the ball, the goalkeeper pulls her arms in to prepare for her landing. Notice that the goalkeeper here has landed on her side and her arms are tucked in. She then uses the momentum of the landing to roll (Figure C).

on the ground she should roll backward across her back and onto the other shoulder (Figure 27C). If this dive is executed correctly, the goalkeeper should be landing outside the goal. The reason for the roll is to put less pressure on the shoulders during the landing. This roll is only used for penalty strokes, because after the save the play is dead. It is important that your goalkeeper rolls for her safety.

If the ball is sent directly to the goalkeeper, she must get her entire body behind it and drop into a block tackle position (Figure 23) to ensure that the ball will not roll behind her and into the goal.

Drill

Strokes should not be attempted until after your goalkeeper has worked on aerials and dives from the previous chapters. Before practicing strokes, have your goalkeeper stand in her safety crouch and work on extending her arms, pulling them in and rolling. It is hard for goalkeepers to understand "extend, tuck and roll."

Besides placing your goalkeeper on the goal line and having her dive to specific areas, you can also work on her reactionary skills. Have your goalkeeper stand facing a wall. The distance from the wall will be dictated by the goalkeeper's reactive ability. Stand behind your goalkeeper with a tennis ball and throw it at the wall. Have your goalkeeper find the ball and dive to catch it.

Jab Tackle

A jab tackle is used to disturb the ball and to slow down the play when the goalkeeper is shadowing or defending an attacker that is in control of the ball. This is a basic skill that all field players learn, but it is also essential for a goalkeeper to know how to execute. It would be wise to have your goalkeeper practice this skill with her defense. Often a goalkeeper is in a precarious situation where the attacker has a controlled ball and is forcing the goalkeeper to shadow her by moving back and forth across the goal. A goalkeeper is taught to shadow the ball until the right moment appears to execute a skill. When the attacker has the ball in a controlled possession, the goalkeeper is unable to execute a skill. However, by jabbing at the ball, the goalkeeper is able to disturb the control so she can execute a skill of choice.

The goalkeeper should be one stick-length away from the attacker and acting as a defensive player. To execute this skill the goalkeeper loosens her grip on the stick, pushes her arm through her hip with a forceful motion and jabs at the ball, knocking it away from the attacker. Her right hand rotates the stick so that the round side is on the ground and the flat side is up to the sky. Now with a simple movement of the right arm straight out from the hip, she touches the ball. The hand moves from the hip to slightly in front of the body without even stopping her feet and movement with the ball. This movement should be done in a straight line, not a circular motion (Figures 28A, B). The goalkeeper's arm should not leave the side of the body, and her hips should not open up and expose a gap between the legs. She should stay square and move her stick in a front-to-back motion.

This is a difficult skill because it needs to be executed while the goalkeeper is still moving her feet, staying square with the ball, and watching the ball and attacker. Once the ball is jabbed, the attacker becomes startled and must regain possession and control of the ball. At that moment the goalkeeper has the opportunity to decide on what skill to use. It is her choice. She may choose to jab tackle again and force the ball away from the attacker and attempt to do a punch clear to get the ball out, or get her foot in for a nice clear. However, a goalkeeper may see that the attacker is preparing to drive the ball, and in that case, she will need to use a block or slide tackle. Either way, what the goalkeeper wanted to do is accomplished. By executing a little skill, she was able to startle the attacker and execute a big skill to get the ball out and away from the danger zone.

Drill

Cut the tip off a one-foot-tall cone so that a ball will fit on top of it. Place the cone about a stick-length away from your goalkeeper. Place a ball on top of the cone. Have your goalkeeper jog in place in her basic stance, rapidly transferring her weight back and forth. When you blow a whistle or yell "go," the goalkeeper should jab at the bottom of the cone. If the ball falls off the cone, your goalkeeper jabbed hard enough to knock the ball out of the possession of the attacker. Keep an eye on the stick placement while the goalkeeper is jabbing. Also make sure the movement of the stick coming out of the hip, jabbing, then returning to the hip is smooth. In addition, the goalkeeper should continue to move her feet while moving through the jab. For a variation on this drill, line up a bunch of cones in the circle from the top through Zone 2. Have your goalkeeper move and jab at the cones.

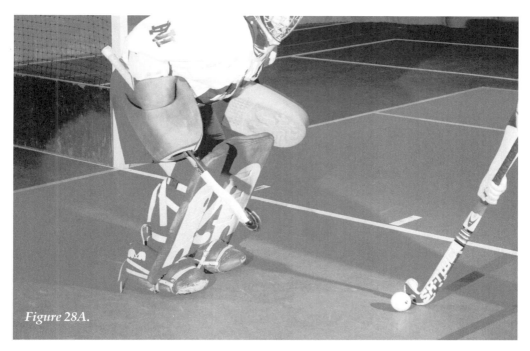

Figure 28A.

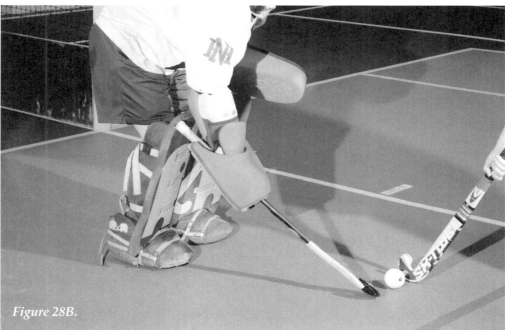

Figure 28B.

Figures 28A-B. The goalkeeper's hand moves out from the hip to the ball, jabbing at the ball. Notice the rotation in the head of the stick and the forward, straight movement of the stick.

chapter 8

Using the Skills – Tactics

This chapter is an attempt to explain what the goalkeeper can do in certain situations. Remember, however, that there isn't only one way to handle these situations. Each team and goalkeeper will handle situations differently depending on the skill level of the players and the styles of team play. This is only a guide for you and your goalkeeper.

One vs. Goalkeeper

In a player-down situation where the goalkeeper is the last defender and must take on a breakaway, the goalkeeper must keep her poise and stand her ground. She must read the attacker and advance to meet her near the top of the circle. She should also communicate to her recovering defenders to mark up as they come down and into the circle. The goalkeeper must stay square and lined up behind the ball. Watch your goalkeeper here and make sure she is aligned with the ball and not the attacker. The goalkeeper should come out of the goal with a hard but controlled run. Don't let the goalkeeper hesitate. The decision must be made quickly and as soon as she sees that her last defender has been beaten.

When the attacker is in the circle and has pulled her stick back, the goalkeeper should freeze to prepare for the shot or to execute a skill. If the goalkeeper is close enough, a block tackle or slide tackle should be executed at this moment. It is important to note that your goalkeeper should not run so hard that she overruns the attacker and takes herself out of play. You don't want your goalkeeper to perform a skill too soon, either. Have her remain poised and watch the ball and the stick of the attacker. Your goalkeeper will need to stay in front of the attacker at a distance of one to two stick-lengths (Figure 28A).

If the attacker enters the circle with her head down and is unaware of her surroundings, the goalkeeper should try to execute a stick dive or slide tackle to retrieve the ball. Make sure that your goalkeeper is aware of where the circle is in relation to her body. She shouldn't be so high that she is playing the ball outside of the circle. If that does happen, however, make sure that she learns to use her stick to sweep the ball toward the closest sideline. Hopefully your goalkeeper has learned enough about distance and timing that this situation will not arise.

If the attacker has her head up and is dribbling with control in the circle, the goalkeeper must shadow her movements until the attacker decides to use a skill. While shadowing the attacker, the goalkeeper can try to jab tackle to force the attacker to do something and to slow down the play. The longer the goalkeeper can prevent the attacker from shooting, the more quickly her defense can recover to help. Remember to make sure that your goalkeeper is square to the ball and prepared for anything. If the ball squeaks past your goalkeeper, it is possible she was lining up with the attacker and not the ball. In addition, make sure that your goalkeeper is using small, quick steps to keep the legs as close together as possible. If she has big bounding steps, the attacker will find a way to send the ball past her. Again, once the attacker is coming down in the hit for a shoot, your goalkeeper will need to stop moving and prepare for the shot. Your goalkeeper will have a better success rate and be able to execute a skill if she is not moving for the shot.

If for some reason the attacker breezes past your goalkeeper — which should not happen if she follows the guidelines I have provided — her recovery should be one of two options. She should either sprint back to the center of the goal and square out to the ball, or sprint back to the center of the goal and use a stick dive as a last ditch effort to try to catch the ball before it crosses the goalmouth.

One vs. Goalkeeper in Zone 3

If the attacker is in Zone 3, tell your goalkeeper to leave her there and not to advance to her. As we discussed in our previous chapter on angles, she doesn't have much of a shot from Zone 3. Have your goalkeeper hold her post and make all clears with the outside leg (the leg that is not on the post). Since the attacker does not have a shot from Zone 3, she will need to pass the ball to Zone 2 or 1. Your goalkeeper will have to judge whether or not she can reach them for an interception. It is important to practice these kinds of cross balls so that your goalkeeper can gauge her range. You will need to practice this with her defense as well, so that they will know what to do and how to help the goalkeeper if she does intercept the ball. If your goalkeeper can't intercept, have her drop step with her outside leg and shuffle across the goalmouth. Make sure the goalkeeper is facing the ball on the shuffle. She will need to creep up to where the ball is in the circle. Work with your goalkeeper and your defense to try to prevent the ball from crossing the field. If the ball crosses to the other side of the field, this will create a shift in the defense and make the goal extremely vulnerable for a shot. Again, this has to be practiced with the defense to find out what works best for you, your team and your goalkeeper.

Two vs. One Defender with Goalkeeper

In a player-down situation in the circle, the goalkeeper must read the play and direct her defense to pressure the ball. The goalkeeper needs to communicate to the defender which direction to force the ball and possibly double-team the ball. When the ball is passed to the open attacker, the goalkeeper then becomes the pressure person and takes her on. The goalkeeper must communicate with her defender so the defender will continue marking while she takes on the attacker with the ball for a one versus goalkeeper. From here the goalkeeper would perform the skills as if it were a true one versus goalkeeper (Figures 29A, B).

This same situation can happen with a recovering defender. The goalkeeper will take on the attacker while communicating with the recovering defender to pick up a mark. When the ball is passed, the defender is now the pressure person and takes on the attacker with the ball. The goalkeeper drops back into the goal and behind the defender for the double-team again.

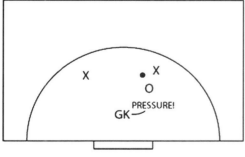

Figure 29A.

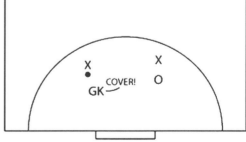

Figure 29B.

Figures 29A-B. When the attacker (X) has the ball, the defender (O) puts pressure on it (Figure A). When the ball is passed to the open attacker (X), the goalkeeper then becomes the pressure person and takes on the attacker with the ball (Figure B).

Cross Balls and End Line Balls

It is essential that your goalkeeper understands her diving range for intercepting balls so that she can be successful. A goalkeeper will need choose which skill is best depending on her range and the distance of the ball, along with the positions of her attackers and defenders. For crossed balls, the goalkeeper can use a lunge, split or stick dive to try to intercept the ball. A dive or lunge save are the two most commonly used on the crossed ball. It is important that your goalkeeper understands her distance ability so that she does not hesitate to perform these skills. A slight hesitation can cause a goal. Practice this situation so she can make a quick and precise decision during a game (Figure 30).

There is another skill for balls that are along the end line which may or may not be crossed. When an attacker is dribbling along the end line, the goalkeeper must hold the post and allow the attacker to come in toward her. This cuts down the attacker's options, as we discussed in previous chapters on angles. The attacker can see very little of the goal and has no choice but to pass the ball. The closer the attacker comes to the goal, the better the chance for the goalkeeper to intercept the ball on the pass. So long as your goalkeeper keeps her post leg on the post and does not allow for a gap, a ball shot from this position has a slim chance of entering the

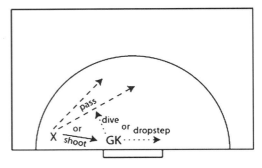

Figure 30. When in Zone 3, X and the goalkeeper have several options. X can shoot on the goal and the goalkeeper can perform a skill. X can also pass the ball to Zones 2 or 1. Depending the distance of the pass, the goalkeeper will need to perform a skill. The goalkeeper can lunge, split or stick dive to intercept the pass. If she cannot intercept the pass, she must drop step, square out to the ball, and prepare for a shot.

goal at this angle. If the ball rebounds off your goalkeeper's pads, she can clear the ball out to the side of the field. However, make sure that she is clearing the ball with her nonpost leg. This is important because if she uses her post leg, she can open a hole to the goal. In addition, if she were to miss the ball using this leg, the ball could go behind her and into the goal. No one wants this to happen, so stress to your goalkeeper the importance of using her outside leg for clears.

All these tactics rely on communication, confidence and knowledge of the techniques and the skills of the game. That is why it is essential that you work closely with your goalkeeper in game-like situations with her defense. The defense and goalkeeper need to understand and trust each other and be able to work together. If they can do this, they will be successful at winning the ball in the circle.

chapter 9

Conclusion

I hope this book provides helpful information for you and your goal-keeper. Basic skills are the essential part of any sport. Once the core skills have been taught, it is up to the athlete to make them their own and transform the movements into second nature. With hard work and desire, a dream can become reality. As I have shown you, a goalkeeper needs to possess more than a love of the game. She must have excellent physical and mental qualities to succeed. You and your goalkeeper now have the knowledge to execute the proper techniques, types of specialty skills, and positions to succeed. I have given you the photographs, explanations and drills to get you and your goalkeeper started.

These basic skills are a guide so that your goalkeeper can have the core knowledge to advance to a higher level of play. These skills cannot be maintained without drills to enhance good body balance and fast footwork in the execution of the techniques. The three Appendices included in this book will help you work with your beginner/intermediate·goalkeeper and your team. Try making some of your own variations on these drills so that they better fit your team and what you are trying to accomplish. As I mentioned previously, each goalkeeper, team and situation is different and situations change in games. These drills are just examples and guides to get you started.

Someone once told me that it takes a million touches to perfect a skill, so practice makes perfect. Keep practicing hard, and you will see results soon.

Footwork Drills

These drills are to be done in three sets of 30-60 seconds each. Only your goalkeeper can determine the intensity level at which she wants to perform. You and your goalkeeper will have to determine the required seconds. I usually do 30 seconds for my beginner goalkeepers. The goalkeeper's rest between drills is just as important. If she works 30 seconds on the drill, she should have 30 seconds or more to rest. These drills are very tiring, so only a few should be done each day. Vary the footwork drills so you don't bore your goalkeeper. These drills are designed to work the feet for a quick change of direction while maintaining balance and control. Make sure that your goalkeeper is in her basic stance and that her head is level throughout the drill. She should make sharp and explosive turns and maintain her basic form throughout each drill. In addition, these drills can be done in or out of equipment.

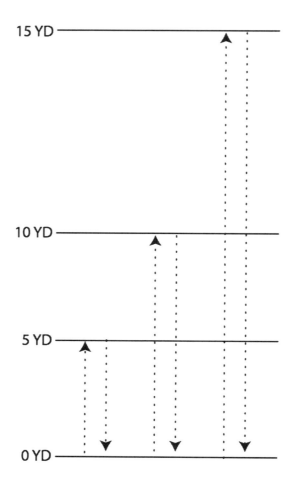

Figure 1: Suicide Sprints

- 5 yards up and back
- 10 yards up and back
- 15 yards up and back
- Use the inside of the circle as a reference for yards for these runs
- Variations include using side slides and backpedals
- Keep the body low

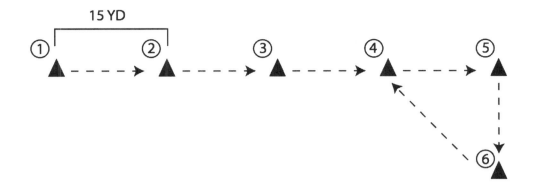

Figure 2: Sprint Through Cones

- At each cone, breakdown (Note: if your goalkeeper is having problems with this, have her say "cha-cha-cha" as she moves through the cones)

- Numbers 5 and 6 work the turn-and-sprint concept

- Keep the body low

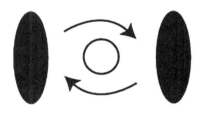

Figure 3: Ball Juggling

- Juggle the ball between the feet, counting consecutive touches

- Work to beat the last goal

- Stay low on the balls of the feet

- Use the stick to punch the ball back between the feet

- Variations include juggling with the stick and one foot only or keeping the ball in the air using the foot, stick, glove, etc.

- Works eye-hand coordination

5 Yards

Figure 4: Side Slides

- Start at one cone and side slide to the other cone and back
- Keep the body low, with shoulders and hips facing forward
- Cross over the cones and touch them
- Explode and change direction

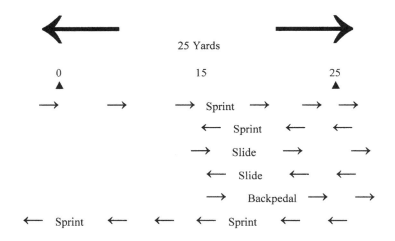

Figure 5: Shuttles

- Start at 0 yards and follow the diagram
- Touch the ground at each destination
- Keep the body low

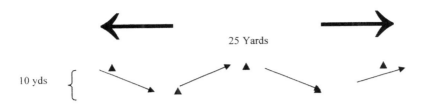

Figure 6: W-Breakdown/W-Run/The Wave

W-Breakdown:

- Start at the end cone
- Accelerate to each cone, breakdown, drop step and sprint to the next cone, etc.
- Stay low and on the toes, pump arms through the run, open hips on the drop step toward the next cone

W-Run:

- Start at the end cone
- Accelerate to each cone and drop step in a continuous run through each cone
- Sprint through the cones, pump arms, stay low and on the toes, open hips on drop step and turn

The Wave:

- Start at the end cone
- Sprint, backpedal, sprint, backpedal through the cones

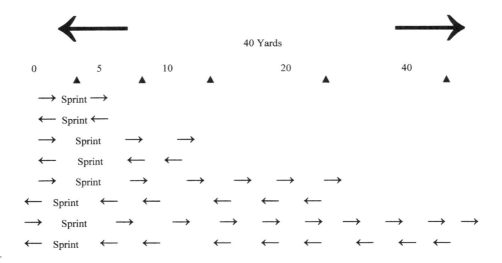

Figure 7: Ladder Sprints

- Start at 0

- Sprint 5 yards and back

- Sprint 10 yards and back

- Sprint 20 yards and back

- Sprint 40 yards and back

- Variations include adding weaves, changing to side slides, putting slide tackles into each cone, having ball pick up and drop stations, etc.

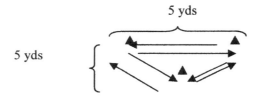

Figure 8: Defensive Slides

- Side slide 5 yards to one cone

- Drop step, side slide 5 yards to the next cone then return sliding through each cone in sequence

- Stay low and on the toes

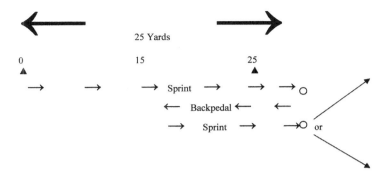

Figure 9: Ball Chase

- Sprint with ball in hand for 25 yards
- Place the ball on the ground at the 25-yard cone then backpedal 10 yards
- Sprint to the ball, pick it up, and run on a 45-degree angle 10 yards

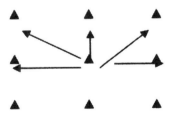

Figure 10: Spider

- Begin at center cone
- Facing forward, sprint or slide to each cone
- Vary your pattern

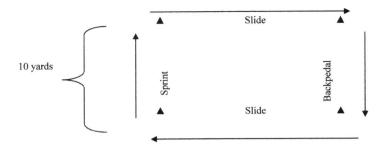

Figure 11: Box Drill

- Start on a corner cone and sprint to another cone; side slide to the next, backpedal to the next, and side slide back to the start

- Change directions if needed

- This can also be done by replacing side slides with lunges

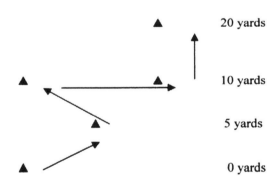

Figure 12: Cone Drills

- Start at the bottom cone

- Sprint through cones 1-3, side slide across to cone 4, and sprint up to the top cone

- Keep focused, stay low, pump arms in run

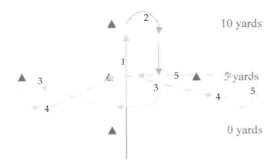

Figure 13: T-Test

- Follow line 1 and sprint to the far cone
- Follow line 2 around the cone and backpedal to the center cone
- Follow line 3 around the cone, side sliding to the left cone and around
- Follow dashed line 4, side sliding across to the right cone and around
- Follow line 5, side sliding back to the center cone and backpedal to the start line

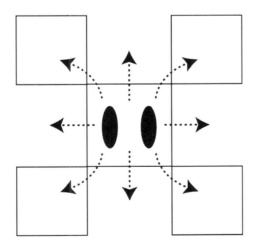

Figure 14: Jump Drill

- Start in the middle
- Jump back and forth between squares, returning to the middle after each jump
- Stay low and in the basic stance

Goalkeeping Drills

This section focuses on goalkeeping drills, although some of the drills also include the entire team. Remember that even when you are working these drills with the team, there are certain things you will need to emphasize for your goalkeeper. Before each team drill, review what you would like your goalkeeper to focus on. The majority of these drills are explained only working one side of the goalkeeper. Please remember when doing a drill to work both sides of the goal and body.

Drills for your Goalkeeper

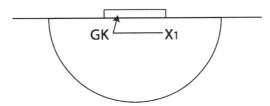

Figure 1: Crossovers/Redirects

Player X sends the ball by push pass or hit to the goalkeeper. The goalkeeper works on crossovers and redirects into the goal. Balls should be placed at the 5-yard hash end line area outside the goal. Switch sides to work on both legs.

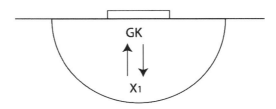

Figure 2: Reaction Shots

The goalkeeper sprints 5-7 yards toward X at the top of the circle, then backpedals. When the goalkeeper is in a backpedal, X shoots the ball.

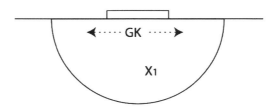

Figure 3: Shuffle Shots

The goalkeeper shuffles from post to post. X sends at the 9-yard line. Every time the goalkeeper is in the center of the goal, X shoots the ball to the goalkeeper.

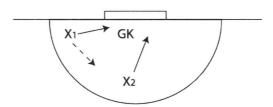

Figure 4: Zone 3 Shots

X1 can pass to X2 or shoot at the goalkeeper from Zone 3. The goalkeeper must try to intercept the pass or deflect the shot over the end line or in a space. Emphasize using nonpost leg for clears.

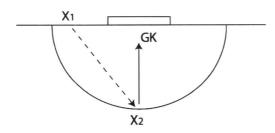

Figure 5: Corner Simulation

X1 and X2 are in a corner formation. X2 shoots to the goalkeeper. The goalkeeper can either practice like a corner or practice ball-moving from Zone 3 to Zone 1 and move along the angles.

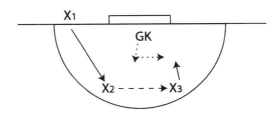

Figure 6: Zone 1 Movement

X1, X2 and X3 are in a corner formation. X1 passes the ball to X2, X2 passes to X3. X3 shoots the ball. The objective here is to get the goalkeeper moving. Practice like a corner or practice ball-moving from Zone 3 to Zone 1 and move along the angles.

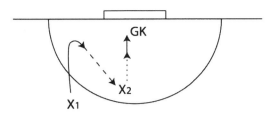

Figure 7: Shots from the Top

X1 starts with the ball outside the circle, dribbles to the end line and curves the ball in toward the center of the goal. Then X1 passes to X2. X2 receives the ball on the move for a quick shot.

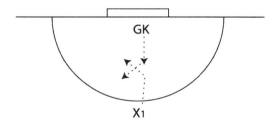

Figure 8: One vs. GK

X starts outside the circle and advances toward the goalkeeper. The goalkeeper begins advancing toward X. When X pulls to the side of the goalkeeper, the goalkeeper does a stick dive on the 45-degree angle, cutting off X. Work both sides. Focus on one versus one. For a variation of this drill, add shadowing skills with jab tackles and slide tackles.

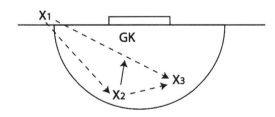

Figure 9: Shot Variety and Movement

X1 enters the circle in Zone 3, and X2 and X3 run into the circle to receive a pass from X1. X1 decides who to pass to. X2 or X3 shoot on goal when she receives the ball. X2 and X3 follow the shot to receive the rebound. The goalkeeper tries to intercept the pass. If she cannot, then she should move along her angle. Have X2 and X3 vary the shots (for example, X2 shoots on goal or passes to X3 and X3 flicks or lifts the ball on goal).

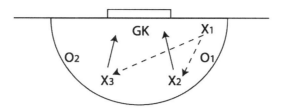

Figure 10: Zone 3 Movement

X1 starts on the end line inside the circle and passes to X2 or X3. X2 or X3 shoots on goal. Goalkeeper must clear to O1 or O2. To vary the drill, have X1 dribble into the circle and pass to X2 or X3, or have X2 and X3 receive the ball on the move as running into the circle, or have X2 and X3 run in for a tip or to catch the rebound off the other attacker's shot.

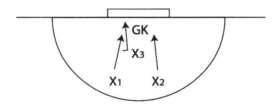

Figure 11: Zone 1 Movement

X1 and X2 dribble around the circle and shoot on goal. The objective is to make the goalkeeper move, so make sure X1 and X2 are very active. X3 tries to tip the ball past the goalkeeper and into the goal. The goalkeeper may need to lower her body to see around or past X3. To vary this drill, add a defender and have the goalkeeper choose for the defender to go get ball or play the tipper.

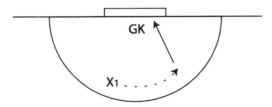

Figure 12: Zone 2 Shots

X dribbles to Zone 2 and shoots. Vary the distances in Zone 2 and the types of shots.

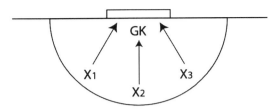

Figure 13: Shot Variation

X1, X2 and X3 take turns shooting on goal. The goalkeeper must clear to the sides and not back to the Xs. Vary the types of shots.

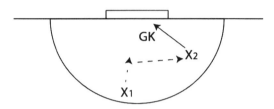

Figure 14: Pull Shots

X1 dribbles into the circle and passes to X2, who is running into Zone 2 of the circle. X2 receives ball and shoots. Have your goalkeeper work on advancing to the ball and performing a slide tackle, freezing for a shot, or moving along her angle. Vary speeds, types of shots and vision on the ball so that your goalkeeper will learn when to run out for a tackle, when to hang back and be patient for the shot, and how to move on her angle.

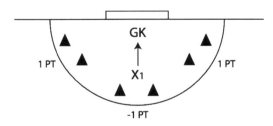

Figure 15: Control Clears

X shoots the ball to the goalkeeper. The goalkeeper must open her hips and try to put the ball between the cones on the sides of the circle. She receives a point for every ball that goes between the cones on the sides, and she loses a point for every ball that she returns up the middle to the attacker. Make this more challenging by having players stand where the side cones would be. Each player would have three colored cones. The goalkeeper would have to say the color as she is clearing the ball to the player.

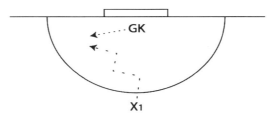

Figure 16: One vs. GK Movement

X1 dribbles into the circle, pulls right or left, accelerates and then pulls right or left. The goalkeeper must advance and shadow and try to stick dive on the pull. Make sure the goalkeeper is on a 45-degree angle, cutting off the attacker during the stick dive.

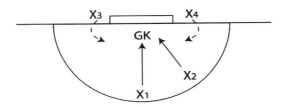

Figure 17: 50/50 Balls

The goalkeeper starts on her stomach and X1 starts with the ball. X1 shoots on goal. The goalkeeper has to watch the player and the ball. When the shot is made, she must get up to perform a skill on the ball. X2 quickly sends an aerial to the goal and the goalkeeper must clear the ball. X3 quickly sends a rolled ball from somewhere behind the goal. The goalkeeper runs on to it like it's a 50/50 ball for a punch clear.

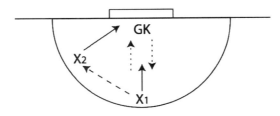

Figure 18: Shots from the Top

The goalkeeper must sprint up seven yards and then backpedal. When in the backpedal, X1 can either shoot on goal or pass to X2 and have X2 shoot on goal. The goalkeeper must focus on performing a skill from a not-so-perfect position (for example, in the middle of a backpedal).

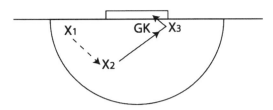

Figure 19: Far Post Shots

X1 stands near the corner hash mark and sends the ball to X2. X2 tries to one time it in on goal. X3 tries to tip it in.

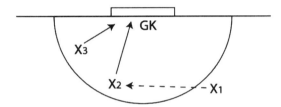

Figure 20: Aerial Shots

X1 passes to X2 for a shot on the far corner of the goal. The goalkeeper dives or splits to save the ball. X3 sends an aerial to the goal. The goalkeeper must quickly get up and play the aerial. To vary this drill have X2 and X3 rush after the aerial and play it out.

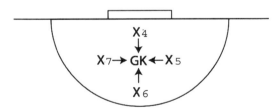

Figure 21: Reaction Drill

The Xs stand in a square about 2 to 3 yards around the goalkeeper. X1 starts with the ball and sends a push pass to the goalkeeper. The goalkeeper faces X1 and reacts to the ball. Once the ball is cleared, X2 push passes the ball to the goalkeeper. The goalkeeper must turn and react to ball. The goalkeeper then turns again to face X3, and continues this pattern until she is out of balls. Use approximately 20 balls. Try to make the goalkeeper spin in different directions. To vary this drill, have the Xs say "here." The goalkeeper must turn to the voice and react to the pass. This will develop fast footwork, quick thought, finding the ball quickly, and reactive skills.

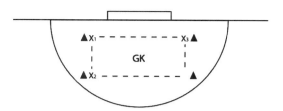

Figure 22: GK in the Middle

Form a 10x10 square around the goalkeeper. Pattern the Xs at the corners of the square, leaving one corner open. The Xs are to pass the ball from corner to corner around the square. The goalkeeper will be in the middle of the square, trying to intercept the ball with a stick dive. Each time an X passes the ball, she must move to an open corner. Every other pass must be on the diagonal. The object of the Xs is to make the goalkeeper move. Once the goalkeeper retrieves the ball, she replaces the X and the X goes in the middle. The goalkeeper will now play like the Xs on the corners, but she will use her feet and work on accuracy. This is a monkey-in-the-middle kind of game that works on flats, throughs, communication on passing and constant movement. The goalkeeper must work on anticipating a pass and intercepting it.

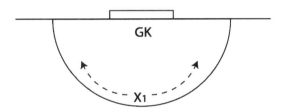

Figure 23: Shots from Zone 2

X dribbles to Zone 2 for shots on goal.

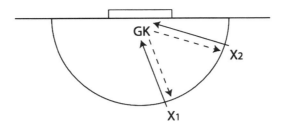

Figure 24: Finding the Space

X1 sends the ball to the goalkeeper and the goalkeeper clears the ball. Do not let the goalkeeper clear the ball back to X1. X2 sends the ball to the goalkeeper and the goalkeeper clears the ball along the end line. Do not let the goalkeeper clear the ball back to X2.

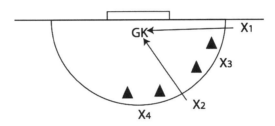

Figure 25: Rebound Shots

X2 push passes the ball to the goalkeeper, and the goalkeeper clears the ball to X1. X2 push passes the ball to the goalkeeper, and the goalkeeper clears the ball to X2. If the ball is cleared to X3 and X4 between the cones, then they can go to goal. The point of this drill is to teach your goalkeeper about accuracy — placing the ball where she wants it and not where the ball ricochets. Variations on this drill include having the goalkeeper aim for X3 and X4 and having them go to goal for a one versus goalkeeper or two versus goalkeeper.

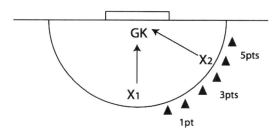

Figure 26: Accuracy Drill

X1 and X2 take turns shooting on goal. The goalkeeper must clear the ball out wide between the cones. There are three gates, each with different point scales: 5, 3, and 1 point(s).

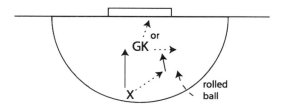

Figure 27: Jab Tackle

X starts with the ball and flicks or lifts it to the goalkeeper. The goalkeeper makes the save. X runs to the goalkeeper where a ball is rolled in to her. X receives the ball on the move and dribbles right/left, trying to dodge the goalkeeper. The goalkeeper must only perform a jab tackle.

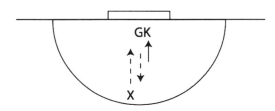

Figure 28: Unexpected Shots

X starts with the ball and dribbles forward to the goalkeeper. The goalkeeper sprints toward X. X pulls the ball back and shoots. The objective is to try to catch the goalkeeper off guard, and to help her get used to making saves for unexpected shots.

Team Training with the Goalkeeper

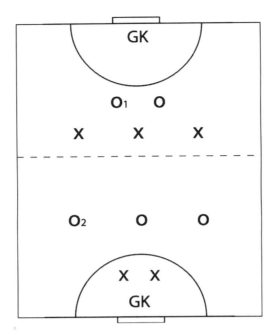

Figure 29: Three vs. Two Continuous

O1 starts with the ball and passes to O2 on the other side of the 25-yard line. O1 cannot crossover to play with O2. O2 and two additional players (O) go to the goal against two defenders (X). This is a three versus two with goalkeeper. If the X team wins the ball, they must pass it to their team on the other side of the 25-yard line, but they may not join. The three Xs now go to goal against the two defenders on the O team. Again this is a three versus two with goalkeeper. The game is now a continuous three versus two with goalkeeper. Play this for 15 minutes and have your goalkeepers work on their one versus one, communication with defense and movement in the goal.

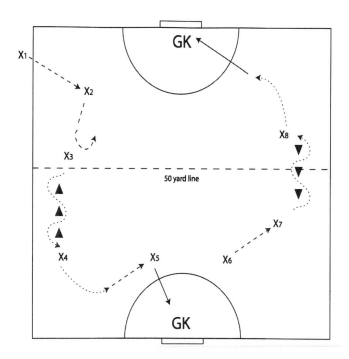

Figure 30: Full Field Team Drill with GK

X1 is at the sideline on one end of the field and push passes to X2. X2 dribbles forward and does a spin. (If your players are not advanced enough for a spin, add a lift here.) After the spin, X2 passes the ball to X3. X3 receives it on the move, weaves through the cones and passes to X4 with a dump ball. X4 runs onto the dump ball pass, dribbles toward the circle entering in Zone 3 and passes to X5. X5 shoots on goal. X6 does a 16-yard hit to X7. X7 receives the ball on the move, weaves and sends a dump ball to X8. X8 runs on the dump ball pass and brings the ball into the circle for a one versus the goalkeeper. Variations of this drill include having X4 and X5 go to goal together and maybe having a defender in there, or having X7 and X8 go to goal together.

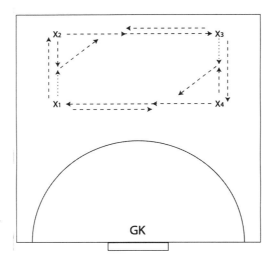

Figure 31: Up Field Movement

X1 passes the ball to X2 and follows her pass. X2 passes the ball back to X1. X2 runs toward X3. X1 passes ball to X2 who is now running to X3. X2 receives the ball on the move and passes to X3. X3 passes back to X2 and runs toward X4. X2 passes the ball to X3. X3 receives the ball on the move and passes it to X4. X4 passes the ball back to X3 and runs toward X1. X3 passes the ball to X4. X4 receives the ball on the move and turns toward the goal. X1 and X2 are now recovering defenders, and X3 and X4 are attackers. Vary the drill by having them move like musical chairs and go to goal when you blow the whistle. The last two players with the ball are the attackers and the other two are the recovering defenders.

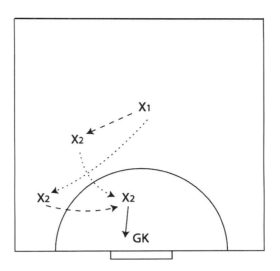

Figure 32: Dump Balls

X1 passes to X2 and X1 runs for a dump ball at the top of the circle in Zone 2. X2 sends the dump ball to X1 and cuts into the circle. X2 can shoot or pass to X1. X2 receives the ball and shoots.

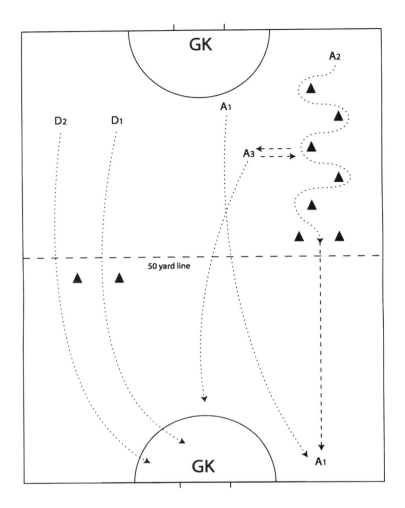

Figure 33: Recovering Defense

A1 passes the ball to A2 and A1 runs to the circle. D1 and D2 run when A1 passes the ball. A2 weaves and passes the ball to A3. A3 bumps the ball back to A2. A2 weaves again and passes the ball to A1. A2 and A3 run to the circle. D1 and D2 are defenders. This will be a three versus two to goal. This drill will work the defense on recovery and teach the goalkeeper to organize as the players run down and into position.

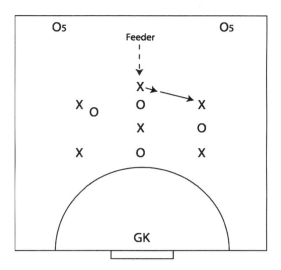

Figure 34: Six vs. Four with GK

A coach or player is the feeder in this six versus four game. O5 on both sides of the field are outlets for the O team defense. Xs are attackers. Work on organization in the circle and team communication for setting up before entering the circle.

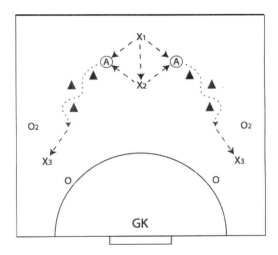

Figure 35: One vs. One with GK

X1 starts with the ball and passes it to X2 for a bump pass back. X1 runs to either the right or left side of the field to A. X1 weaves and passes the ball to X3. X1 and X3 go to goal. O is the defender making this a two versus one with a goalkeeper. O2 is an outlet for O. The goalkeeper and defense should work on pressure/cover communication and trying to isolate the play to a one versus one.

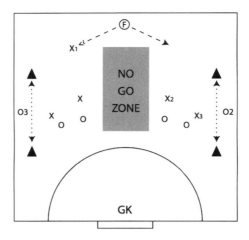

Figure 36: Circle Organization

A coach or player is the feeder in this three versus two game. The feeder passes to either side to any X. Xs go to the goal against O. The O defense can outlet the ball to O3 or the feeder. However, neither team can enter the middle of the field. Vary this by adding more players or moving the game closer to the circle. Work on organization in the circle and team communication for setting up before entering the circle.

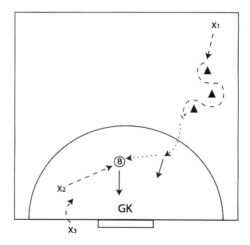

Figure 37: Shot Variety

X1 starts with the ball and dribbles through the cones and into the circle. X1 shoots on goal at the top of the circle. X1 runs to B after the shot for a pass from X2. X1 shoots on goal. X3 runs toward the goalkeeper and X3 tosses a ball in from behind the goal. X1 and the goalkeeper scramble for the ball. X1 shoots if she receives it, or the goalkeeper punch clears the ball out. Work with your attackers to vary their shots here not only for your goalkeeper, but also for your attackers' versatility.

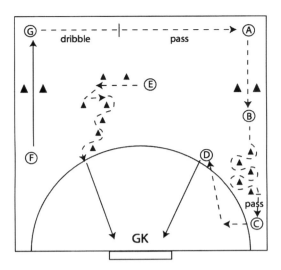

Figure 38: Full Field Drill with Shots on GK

Player X starts at point A and passes to B through the cones. B then weaves through the cones and pushes to C. C hits to D. D receives the ball on the move and shoots. With a new ball, E does a series of pulls and weaves through the cones and shoots. You can stop the drill here or add another component. Have the goalkeeper aim for F. F receives the ball from the goalkeeper and passes the ball up field to G. G dribbles and passes to A. Have your attackers rotate by following their passes. A variation on this drill is to also put a defender in against D or to have F and G work together building up field to the goal.

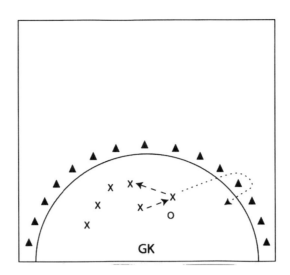

Figure 39: Defense and Fitness Drill

Place cones outside the circle about five yards apart. Start with six at-tackers (X), one defender and a goalkeeper. The Xs are to pass the ball around in the circle. After each pass they must run around a cone before they can receive the ball again. The defense (GK and O) must win the ball three times before they can rotate out of the drill. This is a basic keep-away drill that will work all members of your team. Your Xs will have to communicate in the circle as to who can receive the ball, and your goalkeeper and defender will have to work together to try to win the ball. Timing on the passes and the movement of the ball are extremely important here. Vary this drill by increasing the numbers of players or decreasing the size of the space.

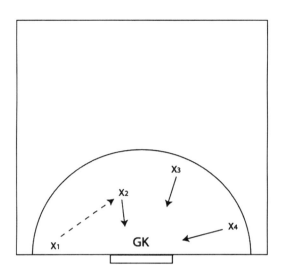

Figure 40: Lift Balls

X1 starts with the ball and passes to X2 or X3 for the shot. If X2 receives the ball, she shoots. If X3 receives the ball, she must flick or lift the ball to goal. If X2 shoots, then X3 still lifts the ball to goal. X4 dribbles to goal and shoots after the goalkeeper plays X3's lift.

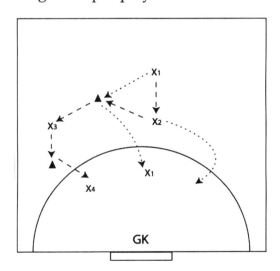

Figure 41: Shot Variety with Attacker Movement

X1 starts with the ball and passes to X2. X1 runs to the cone. X2 passes the ball to X1 who receives it on the move. X2 turns and runs to the circle. X1 passes the ball wide to X3, then runs to support the pass. X3 passes the ball to X4. X4 cuts in off the end line and receives the ball on the move. X4 either passes back to X3, X1 or X2. Then the Xs go to goal.

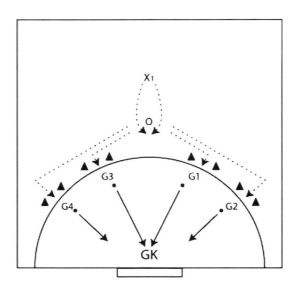

Figure 42: Gate Shots

X1 starts with the ball and dribbles around the center cone and proceeds to gate 1, 2, 3 or 4 for a shot on goal. After each shot, X runs into the circle to flick the loose balls placed there. Have Xs vary the shots.

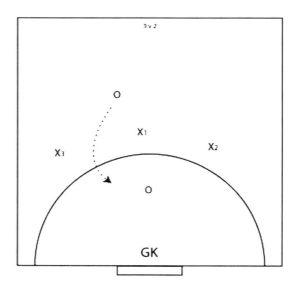

Figure 43: Three vs. Two

Set up a game of three versus two toward the goal, with three Xs outside the circle and one defender in the circle. Position your other defender up field with the Xs. This defender will be recovering. Have your goalkeeper work on positioning defenders and communication during play.

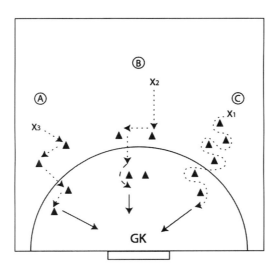

Figure 44: Shot Variety

Have three lines of attackers set up at A, B and C. Section A does a series of pulls and shoots on goal. Section B does a series of pulls, lifts the ball over a log and takes on the goalkeeper, one versus goalkeeper. Section C weaves and shoots on goal. Variations of this drill include changing the type of shots on goal at each section or changing the obstacle that each section has to overcome.

Evaluation Form

The following is an evaluation form that the goalkeepers will work to-gether to fill out. The backup goalkeeper will have several of these forms at each game to evaluate the starting goalkeeper. The backup goalkeeper will evaluate each shot, make comments where suggested and work with the starting goalkeeper to improve her skills. There will also be room for the starting goalkeeper to write down her comments, or she may fill out her own evaluation form. From these evaluations, each goalkeeper can see the skills that need to be improved to make them better goal-keepers and a stronger team. This evaluation form is designed to be a peer- and/or self-evaluation form. It will not be filled out by coaches; however, I do suggest that coaches sit down with their goalkeepers to discuss these evaluation forms. This will help coaches prepare drills to target and strengthen the goalkeeper's weak areas. Coaches should dis-cuss with the goalkeeper what she may have learned from the evalua-tion forms, and what areas of weakness the drills should target to make her stronger in her position.

Goal Evaluation Form

NAME:_____ DATE:_____

Shot

Game_____ **Time**_____ **Score**_____

Type of Shot   **Where Did the Shot Beat Me?**

Chip
Slap
Drive
Push
Lift
Tip
Penalty

Shooter

Shooter   **Situation:**_____
Zone 1   _____
Zone 2   _____
Zone 3   _____

Attack   **Comments:**_____
3v2   _____

3v1 or 3vGK   _____

2v1 or 2vGK   _____

1v1 or 1vGK   _____

Positioning

Position: Save Attempted:
Down   Glove Save   Clear
Up   Stick Save   Block Tackle
                   Slide Tackle   Split
                   Jab

Where Was I?

Ball Movement

What Were the Movements of the Ball?

Comments:_____

_____

_____